KUWAIT AND THE GULF

KUWAIT AND THE GULF

Small States and the International System

Hassan Ali Al-Ebraheem

CENTER FOR CONTEMPORARY ARAB
STUDIES, *Washington, D C*

CROOM HELM
London & Canberra

© 1984 Hassan Ali Al-Ebraheem
Croom Helm Ltd, Provident House, Burrell Row,
Beckenham, Kent BR3 1AT

Croom Helm Australia, PO Box 391,
Manuka, ACT 2603, Australia

British Library Cataloguing in Publication Data

Al-Ebraheem, Hassan Ali
   Kuwait and the Gulf.
   1. States, Small   2. International relations
   3. Persian Gulf Region—Foreign relations
   I. Title
   327'.0953'6   DS326
   ISBN 0-7099-0527-0

First published in the United States of America 1984

Library of Congress Catalog Card Number 83-72166
ISBN 0-932568-08-4

Printed and bound in Great Britain

CONTENTS

ACKNOWLEDGEMENTS

I am deeply indebted to the Center for Contemporary Arab Studies of Georgetown University, Washington, DC, where I enjoyed every courtesy as a Visiting Scholar. Dr Peter F. Krogh, Dean of the University's School of Foreign Service, Dr Michael C. Hudson, the Center's director, and Dr Hisham Sharabi were always supportive of my efforts. The Kuwait University Office in Washington, DC made my stay in Washington a pleasant one. Dr Saif Abdulla, Director of the Kuwait University Office, and Dr Richard Stevens, Assistant Director, extended their official and personal assistance. J. Coleman Kitchen, Jr, the Center's copyeditor, provided a carefully and thoughtfully edited manuscript for final publication. Huda Ajlouni and Mercedes Infante prepared early drafts of the manuscript with great patience and care, and Jeane Tarabulsi assisted with the editing and typing. Dr Sharabi, Dr Stevens, and Dr George Abed read and commented upon the manuscript. I am also grateful to the Library of Congress, which provided research assistance and facilities.

Hassan Ali Al-Ebraheem
Kuwait

INTRODUCTION

One of the major events of the twentieth century has been the emergence of numerous newly independent small states. Many of these new states have found that it is easier to win independence than to achieve national integration, and are beset by administrative and resource problems. Often, their history since independence has been characterized by civil wars, political instability, and economic stagnation. In their efforts to combat economic ills, the leaders of these countries have generally been forced to swing from socialist economics to free enterprise and capitalistic policies. In many cases, hasty and sometimes ruinous economic decisions have led to massive indebtedness, which in turn has resulted in even more distorted policies. 'In Egypt and other Third World societies caught in the debt trap (Peru, Zaire, Turkey, to name a few), the result will be to sacrifice their economic autonomy. In country after country, the "politics of credit worthiness" has more to say about the actual conduct of policy than any ideological exhortations. The crisis of foreign debt brings in its train new forms of intervention and dependence.'[1]

This book is about small states in general, but it focuses on the Gulf region, where a number of small states share a very narrow body of water. This volatile area was ruled for many years by a colonial power which was able, through the use of force, to impose peace until it withdrew. Endowed with precious natural resources, the region now finds itself rent by internal territorial and ideological conflicts and threatened by superpower competition. This study will assess the prospects of the states of this region.

Chapter 1 briefly reviews various key trends that have shaped and changed the international system since World War II, including imperialism, the proliferation of small states, North-South tensions, and changing relations within and between the traditional blocs. Chapter 2 surveys the literature on small states and discusses various definitions of a 'small state.' Chapter 3 examines the role played by the small states in the United Nations. The economies, foreign policies, and security of small states are treated in Chapter 4. Questions are posed concerning the viability of these small states and their dependence upon larger

1

states. Chapters 5 and 6 are concerned with the security of the Arab Gulf states and their attempts to guarantee their survival and viability by integrating themselves in a larger unit. Chapter 7 looks at Kuwait, which has survived for more than 200 years. In its quest for security through integration with the other Gulf states, Kuwait might serve as a model for other small states. Chapter 8 presents some conclusions about the role and prospects of small states and in particular the Gulf countries.

Note

1. F. Ajami, 'Retreat from Economic Nationalism: The Political Economy of Sadat's Egypt,' *Journal of Arab Affairs*, Vol. 1, No. 1 (Oct. 1981), p. 44.

1 THE INTERNATIONAL SYSTEM: THE CHANGING SCENE

'Family of nations,' 'world community,' 'international society' — these are all familiar terms. The concept of the world as an 'international system,' however, is a relatively new one only recently introduced into the field of international politics; this idea reflects the significant changes that have taken place in the international arena since the end of World War II as well as the desire of scholars to utilize a more scientific method involving more precise and quantitative measurements. This chapter will describe the major features of the current international system, characterized as it is by imperialism, the growing number of new states, efforts toward political and economic integration, polarization, proxy war, growing economic inequalities between the 'have' and 'have-not' states, and power diffusion within the traditional blocs. Through an examination of these trends we may better understand how a small state such as Kuwait interacts with the changing international system.

Imperialism

Imperialism — cultural, economic, political and militaristic — has been a part of the international system for a long time. Although there have been many attempts to justify imperialism in the past, the smaller states consider it the cause of many of the world's tragedies, including much of their own economic and political predicament today. The rationale for empire building used by the United States is particularly illustrative, since, as William Appleman Williams notes, it was predicated

> upon a charming but ruthless faith in infinite progress fueled by endless growth. Hence, empire is a way of life projected beyond the continent to the world. Growth is the key to individual liberty and progress. The substance of growth is empire. Thus empire is benevolent. Hence the policeman who guarantees the growth of the law and order that is necessary to progress is undeniably benevolent.[1]

Despite the widespread decolonization that has occurred since 1940, imperialism still exists, but now operates in the economic arena. Economic imperialism is the effort by one country to achieve economic domination and control over another. The best example of this new kind of imperialism is the economic control exercised by the United States over many other countries. This form of imperialism, also called neo-colonialism, is best described as:

> A policy . . . designed to prevent the newly independent countries from consolidating their political independence and thus to keep them economically dependent and securely in the world capitalist system. In the pure case of neo-colonialism the allocation of economic resources, investment effort, legal and ideological structure, and other features of the old society remain unchanged — with the single exception of the substitution of 'internal colonialism' for formal colonialism, that is, the transfer of power to the domestic ruling classes by their former colonial masters. Independence has thus been achieved on conditions which are irrelevant to the basic needs of the society, and represents a part-denial of real sovereignty, and a part-continuation of disunity within the society. The most important branch of the theory of neo-colonialism is therefore the theory of economic imperialism.[2]

Kwame Nkrumah gave one of the most widely accepted definitions of neo-colonialism:

> The essence of neo-colonialism is that the state which is subject to it is, in theory, independent and has all the outward trappings of international sovereignty. In reality its economic system and thus its internal policy is directed from outside.[3]

New States

One of the most important features of the international system is the ever-increasing number of states — large, medium, and small. More than 50 new states joined the international system between 1947 and 1970, and by 1980 the number had increased to 91 (see Table 1.2 at the end of this chapter). Many of these states were born out of imperialistic colonial empires, dismantled in part through the United Nations and its Resolution 1514 (XV) of December 15, 1960. Entitled 'Declaration on the Granting of Independence to Colonial Countries and Peoples,' it reads:

1. The subjection of peoples to alien subjugation, domination and exploitation constitutes a denial of fundamental human rights, is contrary to the Charter of the UN and is an impediment to the promotion of world peace and cooperation.
2. All peoples have the right to self-determination; by virtue of that right, they freely determine their political status and freely pursue their economic, social and cultural development.
3. Inadequacy of political, economic, social or educational preparedness should never serve as a pretext for delaying independence.

Despite the Declaration, independence for many of these new states has been fraught with disappointment and discord. Between 1947 and 1981, for example, civil wars took place in Sudan, Ethiopia, Cyprus, Lebanon, Zaire, Nigeria, Pakistan, and Chad. Major wars have broken out between India and Pakistan, Iraq and Iran, Israel and the Arab countries. Numerous border disputes have included hostilities between Iraq and Kuwait, Algeria and Morocco, Mauritania and Morocco, and Somalia, Kenya, and Uganda.

Political analysts have had differing views about the proliferation of small states. While some have subscribed to the traditional idealization of the small state, others have been unsympathetic to the rise in their numbers, a development, they feel, which runs contrary to the more desirable modern trend toward internationalism and the creation of larger units.[4]

Integration

Integration, a process whereby states are unified into more extensive units, is an important feature of the modern international system, especially with respect to some of the older and larger states. It is not always a deliberate process and has more often occurred in response to the exigencies of the moment. Using the unification of western Europe as an example, E. Haas argues that international integration has often resulted from indirection, trial and error, miscalculation, and manipulation.[5] C. J. Friedrich, commenting on the federalizing process of European unification, has noted that even very loose bonds may have high significance, and that a federal relationship can succeed even if the states involved do not formally renounce a substantial part of their sovereignty or make their membership irrevocable. 'It is possible,' Friedrich continues, 'to let such a relationship evolve, and to solve specific problems as they emerge.'[6]

Many states integrate to increase their economic security. The importance of political sovereignty may decrease given a strong desire by leaders to achieve and sustain high economic growth. Thus, Harold and Margaret Sprout suggest that a trend toward integration can be interpreted as a response by political leaders to domestic constituency pressures for improvements in domestic welfare.[7]

States are further encouraged to integrate because of the revolutionary developments in the field of weaponry. Indeed, it can be argued that this revolution has rendered useless the concept of the traditional nation-state as a protector of its own citizens. For a state to be able to compete in the arms race and protect itself, it has to integrate itself into a larger unit with more resources at its disposal. Friedrich sums up the reasons for the unification of western Europe by saying that Europe, 'formerly the Hub of the Universe,' is 'now being united not only by its defense needs, but by the economic problems which the disintegration of its several colonial empires has created.'[8]

Polarization

The fourth feature of the changing international system is the polarization of the major powers into blocs. The new system — unlike that which existed before World War II — is divided between two major blocs headed by the United States and the Soviet Union. The 'cold war' between the two superpowers has resulted in the most massive arms race in history, which is both a consequence and an important rationale of polarization. This dangerous cycle of tension and weapons production has resulted in more than $300 billion being spent each year in the armaments race. According to the Stockholm International Peace Research Institute, '. . . world military expenditure is greater than either world expenditure on education or health; it is some fifteen times larger than official aid provided to the underdeveloped countries; and it is equivalent to the combined gross national product of all the countries in Africa, the Middle East and South Asia.'[9] In 1978, total world military expenditures amounted to $500 billion; many poor or developing countries spent more on the military than in either the health or education sectors. Table 1.1 illustrates the world's per capita spending priorities in 1978 US dollars.

The nuclear arms race is a key component in polarization and an important and dangerous feature of the contemporary international system in its own right. H.F. York argues that both superpowers have already reached the point where they can destroy each other:

It is most important . . . to have clearly in the mind what the current technical situation means: the survival of the combined populations of the superpowers depends on the good will and the good sense of separate leaderships of the superpowers. If the Soviet leadership, for whatever reason, or as a result of whatever mistaken information, chose to destroy America as a nation, it is unquestionably capable of doing so in less than half an hour, and there is literally nothing we could now do to prevent it. The only thing we could do is wreak on them an equally terrible revenge. And of course, the situation is the same the other way around.[10]

Nuclear war would not, of course, be limited to the two powers but would devastate areas far from the warring nations:

In addition, the lives of many millions of people living in the immediate neighborhood of the superpowers would be imperiled by the so-called fallout, and long-range or world-wide fallout would endanger those living in even remote countries. It is very difficult to make precise estimates, but it seems that a full nuclear exchange between the US and USSR would result in the order of 10,000,000 casualties from cancer and leukemia in countries situated well away from the two main protagonists. In addition, genetic problems that are even more difficult would

Table 1.1: The World's Spending Priorities (1978 Per Capita
Expenditures in US Dollars)

	Military	Education	Health
ASIA			
Afghanistan	5	3	1
Australia	207	524	325
Bahrain	141	181	141
Bangladesh	1	2	0.3
Brunei	642	239	N/A
Burma	5	2	1
China	26	15	6
Cyprus	39	75	32
Fiji	12	82	33
India	5	5	2
Indonesia	11	6	5
Iran	261	115	31
Iraq	159	70	11
Israel	839	303	114
Japan	80	489	389
Jordan	87	31	10
Korea, North	63	26	3
Korea, South	75	32	3
Kuwait	613	454	287
Laos	10	2	1
Lebanon	58	N/A	N/A
Malaysia	45	71	20
Mongolia	76	51	10
Nepal	1	2	0.8
New Zealand	93	311	267
Oman	914	94	57
Pakistan	12	5	1
Papua New Guinea	9	42	17
Philippines	11	11	4
Qatar	1194	1990	333
Saudi Arabia	1004	507	137
Singapore	186	84	57
Sri Lanka	1	5	3
Syria	147	55	4
Taiwan	106	55	35
Thailand	18	17	3
United Arab Emirates	836	277	250
Vietnam	18	4	1
Yemen, Arab Rep.	52	10	4
Yemen, People's Dem. Rep.	43	13	5
AFRICA			
Algeria	36	115	18
Angola	—	15	7
Benin	3	11	0.3
Botswana	22	48	15

	Military	Education	Health
Burundi	5	4	1
Cameroon	7	13	4
Cent. African Rep.	4	8	3
Chad	8	3	2
Congo	23	45	10
Egypt	91	28	9
Equatorial Guinea	25	10	4
Ethiopia	5	3	1
Gabon	78	100	48
Gambia	—	11	7
Ghana	5	16	7
Guinea	4	9	3
Ivory Coast	11	64	14
Kenya	12	17	6
Lesotho	—	10	3
Liberia	5	28	11
Libya	156	387	80
Madagascar	6	13	4
Malawi	4	5	2
Mali	4	5	1
Mauritania	30	16	5
Mauritius	2	64	26
Morocco	42	41	8
Mozambique	9	3	2
Niger	2	3	2
Nigeria	28	34	4
Rwanda	3	4	1
Senegal	10	12	4
Sierra Leone	2	9	4
Somalia	12	7	3
South Africa	80	67	6
Sudan	14	4	3
Swaziland	2	38	11
Tanzania	10	12	5
Togo	8	21	7
Tunisia	30	58	24
Uganda	11	10	4
Upper Volta	4	4	1
Zaire	10	6	3
Zambia	41	24	12
Zimbabwe	31	19	9
EUROPE			
Albania	60	31	17
Austria	93	438	376
Belgium	322	589	399
Great Britain	262	297	268
Bulgaria	77	120	65
Czechoslovakia	143	144	137
Denmark	259	752	806
Finland	102	489	318
France	350	512	546
Germany, East	218	226	113
Germany, West	350	491	591

	Military	Education	Health
Greece	220	74	98
Hungary	79	142	93
Iceland	—	397	545
Ireland	59	232	220
Italy	112	215	211
Luxembourg	103	698	103
Malta	24	74	74
Netherlands	304	730	560
Norway	322	729	633
Poland	99	101	113
Portugal	64	73	63
Rumania	56	103	70
Spain	67	86	116
Sweden	365	927	883
Switzerland	280	710	486
Turkey	64	44	10
Soviet Union	394	189	82
Yugoslavia	105	136	100
NORTH AMERICA			
Canada	174	688	469
United States	499	565	341
LATIN AMERICA			
Argentina	55	54	11
Barbados	4	158	70
Bolivia	18	32	8
Brazil	18	55	27
Chile	73	50	34
Colombia	7	20	11
Costa Rica	11	99	19
Cuba	49	82	41
Dominican Rep.	17	18	12
Ecuador	22	35	9
El Salvador	13	23	9
Guatemala	9	14	7
Guyana	10	46	15
Haiti	2	2	1
Honduras	11	18	10
Jamaica	9	79	34
Mexico	8	68	10
Nicaragua	28	24	13
Panama	9	65	60
Paraguay	13	13	3
Peru	33	17	6
Trinidad & Tobago	11	140	63
Uruguay	40	32	20
Venezuela	44	149	83

Source: The *New York Times*, September 20, 1981.

affect many, many millions of others not only in this generation but for centuries to come. Civilization would survive some-where, but probably not in the US or the Soviet Union, and perhaps not elsewhere in North America or Europe.[11]

Something else that is both a source and perhaps the most dangerous consequence of polarization is the acquisition of nuclear technology by more and more states. The monopoly over nuclear power maintained by the United States (1945), the USSR (1949), Britain (1952), France (1960), China (1964), and India (1974), is now being broken by countries that already have nuclear power or are on the threshold of acquiring it. It has been estimated that within the next decade no less than 28 to 30 countries will join the nuclear club. The emergence of so many nuclear powers in the near future will have a profound effect on the character of the contemporary state system.[12]

The Changing Nature of War

While scientific and technical advances have altered the nature of war, nuclear armaments have brought a period of more than 30 years without a world-wide conflict. Although the world has not been free of wars, these wars have been relatively small and limited. A 'balance of terror' of sorts has been imposed upon the superpowers through the development of the nuclear bomb. Not wanting or daring to use it, they have resorted to waging limited wars throughout the world by proxy. Both have deployed their forces on foreign soil and used them as political instruments to further their own interests. Blechman and Kaplan, in their comprehensive work on the US armed forces, conclude that the United States used its forces as a political instrument on 215 occasions during the period from January 1, 1946 through December 31, 1975.[13] In like fashion, the Soviet Union used its armed forces in 190 incidents between June 1944 and August 1979.[14]

Haves and Have-nots

Roger Hansen, writing in *Beyond the North-South Stalemate*, argues that two central rifts mark the international system: the East-West division, based upon differing conceptions of security concerns and societal management, and the North-South division between rich and poor countries.[15] The Third World countries, also known as the Less Developed Countries (LDCs) and the 'Group of 77,'[16] have tried to rectify this gap by cooperating among themselves and by working to bring about North-South negotiations that would lead to a new world economic order to replace the present order which, the LDCs believe, has been structured in favor of the industrial countries. The LDCs — which are expected to contain 79 percent of the world's population by the year 2000 — are a fiercely loyal group, especially in their opposition to the other, more 'developed' groupings of countries. Sharing a common history of exploitation by Western economic interests, the LDCs and the Organization of Petroleum Exporting Countries (OPEC) formed a natural alliance. In 1973-4, the LDCs achieved a major breakthrough in power bargaining and recognition with the success of the Arab oil embargo.

Diffusion of Power

Another major feature of the modern state system is the increased diffusion of power within the two major blocs. There has been a movement away from a strictly bipolar situation and toward the emergence of multipolar groupings within the blocs. France, for example, has pursued independent policies and has encouraged other states to follow suit. Power diffusion is also occurring within the states themselves as a result of a decline in the domestic authority of many governments. Even such 'mature' states as Britain, France, Spain, Belgium, Italy, and Austria must cope with the aspirations of dissatisfied minorities. Diffusion of power has also led to a decline of the Western-dominated economic system based on the Bretton Woods formula, and to stronger Third World demands for a system in which the LDCs would have a larger share.

Second-order Powers

One more significant development in the international system since World War II is the increase in the numbers of so-called 'second-order powers.' This is due to many factors, including political modernization, the diffusion of technology (including nuclear), the armaments race, and the development of internal geopolitical regional linkages (including the possibilities for regional and economic cartels).[17] The struggle of the Third World countries to break away from the economic, political, cultural, and military domination of the larger powers has also contributed to the emergence of second-order powers. Generally characterized by such qualities as strategic position, military and industrial potential, and skilled manpower resources, the second-order powers include: Canada, Mexico, Venezuela, Brazil, Algeria, Austria, Nigeria, South Africa, East Germany, Romania, India, Turkey, Egypt, Israel, Indonesia, Vietnam, Spain, and Yugoslavia.[18]

The Small State in the International System

Although the small state may formally be equal in sovereignty to any other country, there is no question that, in isolation, it is subjected to pressures over which it has little if any control. Frequently forced to accommodate the interests of more powerful states, the small state might find itself obliged to waive import duties on various manufactures in return for markets or budget subsidies, as is the case with many of the francophone states of Africa. The adoption of a particular stance on an issue before the United Nations General Assembly may be the price which a small state has to pay to secure financial assistance or political support. Subjected to sophisticated forms of imperialism, lacking the strong internal structures essential to long-term political stability, and caught up in a world-wide superpower competition for power and influence, the small state of the 1980s finds itself the object of power with little leverage at its disposal. Whether the small states can display sufficient political acumen to forego short-term economic or political gains in order to acquire a more meaningful role in the international system remains to be seen. For the oil-rich Gulf states in particular, the blandishments of security arrangements that might erode domestic popular support of present regimes pose a special challenge and require a proper understanding of the international system today. Some basic facts about that system are presented in Table 1.2.

Table 1.2: The International System 1981

Country	Location	Independence[b]	Square Miles[c] (thousands)	Population[d] (thousands)	Micro	Small	Medium	Large	Diplomatic Missions[f]	US Mission to[g]	Mission to US[h]	UN System	Other
Afghanistan	Asia	*	251.0	17,480			E		46 (19)	X	X	15	0
Albania	Europe	*	11.1	2,734		D			54	*	*	9	1
Algeria	ME	1962	920.0	19,129			E		46 (41)	X	X	16	2
Andorra	Europe	*	(179.0)	35	A				*	*	*	*	*
Angola	Africa	1975	481.4	6,759			E		15	*	*	1	0
Antigua and Barbuda	WH	1981	(171.0)	75,000	A				*	X	*	1	2
Argentina	WH	*	1,065.1	27,064			F		81 (68)	X	X	17	3
Australia	Oceania	*	2,966.0	14,518			E		68	X	X	17	3
Austria	Europe	*	32.4	7,481			E		140 (57)	X	X	16	3
Bahamas	WH	1973	5.4	232	B				2	X	X	8	0
Bahrain	ME	1971	(258.0)	383		C			9	X	X	9	0
Bangladesh	Asia	1972	55.6	88,678				H	71	X	X	14	1
Barbados	WH	1966	(166.0)	249	B				5	X	X	13	1
Belgium	Europe	*	11.8	9,855			E		132	X	X	17	3
Belize	WH	1981	8.9	146,000	B				*	X	X	1	1
Benin	Africa	1960	43.5	3,338		D			14	X	X	14	1
Bhutan	Asia	*	17.8	1,298		D			2	*	*	4	0
Bolivia	WH	*	424.2	5,570			E		19	X	X	14	2
Botswana	Africa	1966	222.0	819		C			4	X	X	9	1
Brazil	WH	*	3,286.5	123,032				I	73	X	X	17	3
Bulgaria	Europe	1948	42.8	8,805			E		100 (59)	X	X	13	2
Burma	Asia	1948	261.8	35,289		F			27	X	X	16	1
Burundi	Africa	1962	10.7	4,110		D			19	X	X	13	2

Byelorussian SSR	Europe	*	80.2	9,002			E	*		*	*	10	1
Cameroon	Africa	1960	179.5	8,444			E	30		X	X	17	2
Canada	WH	*	3,851.8	23,869			E	127		X	X	17	3
Cape Verde Islands	Africa	1975	1.6	296	B			5		X	X	2	0
Central African Rep.	Africa	1960	240.5	2,362		D		21		X	X	13	1
Chad	Africa	1960	495.8	4,504		D		20		X	X	14	1
Chile	WH	*	292.1	11,104				59		X	X	17	3
China, People's Rep.	Asia	*	3,691.5	971,000				97		*	*	5	0
China, Rep. of	Asia	*	13.9	17,704			J	32		X	X	16	2
Colombia	WH	*	439.7	27,326			E	39	(38)	X	X	3	0
Comoros, Rep. of	Africa	1975	(692.0)	300		C	F	1		X	X	14	1
Congo	Africa	1960	132.0	1,537		D		21		*	*	15	1
Costa Rica	WH	*	19.7	2,232		D		19		X	X	13	3
Cuba	WH	*	44.8	9,738			E	51		X	X	17	1
Cyprus	Europe	1960	3.6	621		C		11		X	X	13	3
Czechoslovakia	Europe	*	49.4	15,309			E	88	(70)	X	X	17	3
Denmark	Europe	*	16.6	5,126			E	106	(105)	X	X	*	*
Djibouti	Africa	1977	8.9	315		C		5		X	X	*	*
Dominica	WH	1978	(300.0)	90	A			*		*	*	16	3
Dominican Republic	WH	*	18.7	5,400		D	E	33		X	X	16	2
Ecuador	WH	*	108.6	8,354		C	E	29		X	X	17	3
Egypt	ME	*	385.2	41,065			F	79		X	X	15	2
El Salvador	WH	*	8.1	4,801		D		37	(25)	X	X	9	1
Equatorial Guinea	Africa	1968	10.8	330		C	F	12		X	X	15	0
Ethiopia	Africa	*	471.8	31,065				27		X	X	11	1
Fiji	Oceania	1970	7.1	619		C		5		X	X	17	3
Finland	Europe	*	130.1	4,771		D		92		X	X	17	3
France	Europe	*	210.0	53,752			G	111	(43)	X	X	16	1
Gabon	Africa	1960	103.3	1,300		D		20		X	X	10	1
Gambia, The	Africa	1965	4.1	601		C		6		X	X	11	0
Germany, Democ. Rep.	Europe	1949	41.8	16,740			E	76		X	X	17	3
Germany, Federal Rep.	Europe	*	96.0	61,439			G	112		X	X	17	3

Country	Location	Independence[b]	Square Miles[c] (thousands)	Population[d] (thousands)	Category[e] Micro	Small	Medium	Large	Diplomatic Missions[f]	US Mission to[g]	Mission to US[h]	Int'l Org. Membership UN System	Other
Ghana	Africa	1957	92.1	11,400			E		37	X	X	16	1
Greece	Europe	*	50.9	9,308			E		67 (47)	X	X	17	3
Grenada	WH	1974	(133.0)	110	B				7	X	X	3	0
Guatemala	WH	*	42.0	7,262			E		30 (28)	X	X	15	1
Guinea	Africa	1958	94.9	5,014			E		31	X	X	13	0
Guinea-Bissau	Africa	1974	13.9	777		C			10	X	X	5	0
Guyana	WH	1966	83.0	884		C			10	X	X	14	1
Haiti	WH	*	10.7	4,919		D			24	X	X	15	3
Honduras	WH	*	43.3	3,691		D			21	X	X	15	1
Hungary	Europe	*	35.9	10,710			E		100 (63)	X	X	13	3
Iceland	Europe	1944	39.7	229	B				9	X	X	15	11
India	Asia	1947	1,269.4	683,810				J	118	X	X	17	15
Indonesia	Asia	1949	741.1	147,490				I	63	X	X	16	14
Iran	ME	*	636.0	39,097			F		?	*	*	15	11
Iraq	ME	1932	168.0	12,327			E		48	*	*	16	17
Ireland	Europe	1921	27.1	3,431			E		24	X	X	17	11
Israel	ME	1948	8.0	3,871		D			56	X	X	17	11
Italy	Europe	*	116.3	57,198				G	111	X	X	17	6
Ivory Coast	Africa	1960	124.5	8,574			E		32	X	X	17	21
Jamaica	WH	1962	4.2	2,183	B				15	X	X	16	14
Japan	Asia	*	145.8	117,810				I	108	X	X	17	10
Jordan	ME	1946	36.8	2,152		D			32	X	X	16	18
Kampuchea	Asia	1949	69.8	5,746			E		?	*	*	2	4
Kenya	Africa	1963	224.0	16,572			E		19	X	X	17	7
Kiribati	Asia	1979	(266.0)	58	A				—	*	*	—	8
Korea, Dem.	Asia	1948	47.0	18,348			E		?	*	*	8	3

Country	Region	Year										
Korea, Rep.	Asia	1948	38.0	37,448		F	80		X	X	18	19
Kuwait	ME	1961	6.5	1,463		D	39		X	X	16	8
Laos	Asia	1949	91.4	3,810		D	18		X	X	13	9
Lebanon	ME	1943	3.9	3,238		D	61		X	X	17	5
Lesotho	Africa	1966	11.7	1,373		D	8		X	X	15	5
Liberia	Africa	*	37.7	1,926		D	40		X*	X*	15	7
Libya	ME	1951	675.0	3,250		D	76		*	*	16	9
Liechtenstein	Europe	1866	(62.0)	25	A		0		X	X	3	6
Luxembourg	Europe	*	(999.0)	365		C	11		X	X	19	11
Madagascar	Africa	1960	226.6	8,714		E	12		X	X	16	4
Malawi	Africa	1964	45.7	6,370		E	11		X	X	16	5
Malaysia	Asia	1957	127.3	13,435		E	52		X*	X*	16	10
Maldives	Asia	1965	(115.0)	152	B		1		*	*	13	
Mali	Africa	1960	478.8	6,833		E	20		X	X	15	10
Malta	Europe	1964	(124.0)	344		C	55		X	X	15	5
Mauritania	Africa	1960	398.0	1,600		D	25		X	X	14	4
Mauritius	Africa	1968	(787.0)	995		C	9		X	X	15	2
Mexico	WH	*	761.6	67,405		G	75	(70)	X	X	17	2
Monaco	Europe	*	(0.73)	25	A		*		X	X	X	X
Mongolia	Asia	*	604.0	1,594		D	58		X	X	10	0
Morocco	ME	1956	177.1	19,470		E	35		X	X	17	1
Mozambique	Africa	1975	308.6	12,375		E	4		X	X	3	0
Nauru	Oceania	1968	(8.0)	7	A		*		X*	X*	2	0
Nepal	Asia	1947	56.1	1,401		E	56	(13)	X	X	14	0
Netherlands	Europe	*	15.9	14,091		E	136	(82)	X	X	17	3
New Zealand	Oceania	*	103.8	3,148		D	43		X	X	15	2
Nicaragua	WH	*	49.7	2,732		D	25		X	X	14	3
Niger	Africa	1960	458.1	5,305		E	21		X	X	15	1
Nigeria	Africa	1960	356.7	77,000		G	46		X	X	16	1
Norway	Europe	*	125.1	4,082		D	101	(44)	X	X	17	3
Oman	ME	1970	120.0	891		C	11		X	X	14	0
Pakistan	Asia	1947	307.3	82,441		H	95		X	X	16	3

Country	Location	Independence[b]	Square Miles[c] (thousands)	Population (thousands)	Micro	Small	Medium	Large	Diplomatic Missions[f]	US Mission to[g]	Mission to US[h]	UN System	Other
Panama	WH	*	29.7	1,830		D			53 (36)	X	X	16	2
Papua New Guinea	Oceania	1975	178.7	3,078		D			13	*	X	3	0
Paraguay	WH	*	157.0	3,067		D			25 (22)	X	X	15	1
Peru	WH	*	496.2	17,291			E		61	X	X	16	3
Philippines	Asia	1946	115.8	48,358			F		42	X	X	16	1
Poland	Europe	*	120.7	35,382			F		92	X	X	13	3
Portugal	Europe	*	35.3	9,856			E		47	X	X	15	3
Qatar	ME	1971	4.4	250	B				25	X	X	11	3
Romania	Europe	*	91.7	22,048			E		104	X	X	15	3
Rwanda	Africa	1962	10.2	5,130			E		18	X	X	13	2
Saint Lucia	WH	1979	(240.0)	130	B				3	X	*	*	*
St Vincent & the Grenadines	WH	1979	(150.0)	117	B				2	X	*	*	*
San Marino	Europe	*	(24.0)	21	A					*	*	*	*
Sao Tome & Principe	Africa	1975	(372.0)	85	A				3	X	*	2	0
Saudi Arabia	ME	*	865.0	8,367			E		28	X	X	15	1
Senegal	Africa	1960	76.0	5,661			E		25	X	X	17	2
Seychelles	Africa	1976	(171.0)	63	A					X	*	*	*
Sierra Leone	Africa	1961	27.7	3,474		D			16	X	X	16	1
Singapore	Asia	1965	(238.0)	2,390		D			32	X	X	14	2
Solomon Islands	Oceania	1978	10.6	227	B				*	X	X	*	*
Somalia	Africa	1960	246.3	3,645		D			15	X	X	14	0
South Africa	Africa	*	471.9	27,552			F		25 (22)	X	X	13	2
Spain	Europe	*	194.9	37,272			F		98 (75)	X	X	17	3
Sri Lanka	Asia	1948	25.3	14,871			E		56	X	X	16	2
Sudan	ME	1956	967.0	18,371			E		58 (26)	X	X	17	2

Country	Region	Year	Pop	Area			No.				
Surinam	WH	1975	70.0	389	C		6	X	X	3	0
Swaziland	Africa	1968	6.7	544	C		4	X	X	11	2
Sweden	Europe	*	173.7	8,314		E	127 (72)	X	X	17	3
Switzerland	Europe	*	15.9	6,310		E	120	X	X	12	3
Syria	ME	1944	71.5	8,647		E	53	X	X	17	1
Tanzania	Africa	1961	364.8	17,982		E	63	X	X	15	1
Thailand	Asia	*	209.4	46,113		F	40 (38)	X	X	17	2
Togo	Africa	1960	21.9	2,699	D		14	X	X	15	1
Tonga	Oceania	1970	(290.0)	96	A		*	X	X	2	1
Trinidad & Tobago	WH	1962	2.0	1,156	D		13	X	X	15	1
Tunisia	ME	1956	52.6	6,367		E	36	X	X	17	1
Turkey	ME	*	301.9	45,217		F	61	X	X	17	3
Tuvalu	Oceania	1979	(9.5)	7	A		*	X	*	*	*
Uganda	Africa	1962	93.1	12,600		E	12	*	X	16	2
Ukranian SSR	Europe	*	232.0	47,127		F	*	X	X	10	1
USSR	Europe	*	8,650.0	264,500		J	116 (122)	X	*	12	2
United Arab Emirates	ME	1971	32.3	891	C		38	X	X	12	0
United Kingdom	Europe	*	94.2	55,902		G	134	X	X	17	3
United States	WH	*	3,651.1	223,239		J	131	X	X	17	3
Upper Volta	Africa	1960	105.9	6,908		E	13	X	X	14	2
Uruguay	WH	*	68.0	2,905	D		43	X	X	15	3
Vanuatu	Oceania	1980	4.6	109	B		*	X	*	*	*
Vatican City	Europe	*	(0.17)	0.9	A		77	*	*	3	1
Venezuela	WH	*	347.1	13,913		E	49	X	*	14	2
Vietnam, Soc. Rep. of	Asia	1954	127.2	52,299		F	25	*	X	0	0
Western Samoa	Oceania	1962	1.1	155	B		*	X	*	5	0
Yemen Arab Rep. (San'a)	ME	*	77.2	5,212		E	13	X	X	14	0
Yemen People's Democ. Republic (Aden)	ME	1967	130.5	1,859	D		60	*	X	13	1
Yugoslavia	Europe	*	98.8	22,328		E	92	*	*	17	3
Zaire	Africa	1960	905.3	25,560		F	51	X	X	17	3
Zambia	Africa	1964	290.6	6,027		E	17	X	X	15	1
Zimbabwe	Africa	1980	150.8	7,360		E	9	X	X	X	X

Notes to Table 1.2:

a. Geographic areas include Western Hemisphere (WH), Europe, Mid-East & North Africa (ME), Asia & Indian Ocean (Asia), a Oceania. Locations are based on US Dept. of State and United Nations categorizations.
b. * indicates pre-WW II (1940) independent states.
c. Figures are rounded to nearest 100 sq. miles. Figures in parentheses are specific areas for countries with areas of less than 100 square miles.
d. Indicated in thousands.
e. *Categories*: (A) Micro-states (population under 100,000) (B) Micro-states (100,000–300,000) (C) Small States (300,000–1,000,000) (D) Small States (1,000,000–5,000,000) (E) Medium States (5,000,000–25,000,000) (F) Medium States (25,000,000–50,000,000) (G) Large States (50,000,000–75,000,000) (H) Large States (75,000,000–100,000,000) (I) Large States (100,000,000–200,000,000) (J) Large States (more than 200,000,000)
   All population statistics are taken from the *Encyclopaedia Britannica 1981 Book of the Year*.
f. Figures indicate number of diplomatic missions to other governments headed by ambassadors. In cases of multiple accreditation, the figures in brackets indicate the actual number of embassies which exist. An asterisk indicates unknown.
g., h. An X indicates a residential or non-residential mission. An asterisk indicates the absence of diplomatic relations.

Notes

1. William A. Williams, *Empire as a Way of Life* (Oxford: Oxford University Press, 1981), p. 113.

2. James O'Connor, 'The Meaning of Economic Imperialism,' *Readings in U.S. Imperialism*, eds. K.T. Fann and Donald C. Hodges (Boston: Porter Sargent, 1971), p. 40.

3. Kwame Nkrumah, *Neo-Colonialism: The Last Stage of Imperialism* (New York: International Publishers, 1965), p. ix.

4. For details on this subject, see E.H. Carr, *The Bolshevik Revolution 1917-1923*, Vol. I (New York: Macmillan, 1951), pp. 410-18.

5. E. Haas, *The Uniting of Europe* (Stanford: Stanford University Press, 1968), p. xii. Reissued, with a new preface.

6. C.J. Friedrich, *Trends of Federalism in Theory and Practice* (London: Pall Mall, 1968), p. 159.

7. Harold and Margaret Sprout, 'The Dilemma of Rising Demands and Insufficient Resources,' *World Politics*, 20 (1968), pp. 660-93.

8. Friedrich, *Trends of Federalism*, p. 156.

9. *Stockholm International Peace Research Institute Yearbook*, 1975, p. 100 gives a slightly different version: the figure for the world military expenditure is almost '15 times larger than official aid provided to the underdeveloped countries; and it is equivalent to the combined gross national product' of the developing countries of South Asia, the Middle East, and Africa combined.

10. H.F. York, 'Nuclear Deterrence: How to Reduce the Overkill,' *Pacem in Terris III*, ed. F.W. Neal and M.K. Harvey (Santa Barbara, California: Center for the Study of Democratic Institutions, 1974), Vol. 2, p. 25.

11. J.B. Wiesner and H.F. York, 'National Security and the Nuclear Test Ban,' *Scientific American*, Vol. 229, No. 4 (Oct. 1964), p. 24.

12. For details, see H. Bull, *The Anarchical Society* (London: Macmillan, 1977), pp. 240-3.

13. B.M. Blechman and S.S. Kaplan, *Force Without War: U.S. Armed Forces as a Political Instrument* (The Brookings Institution: Washington, DC, 1978), pp. 547-53.

14. S.S. Kaplan, *Diplomacy of Power: Soviet Armed Forces as a Political Instrument* (The Brookings Institution: Washington, DC, 1981), pp. 689-93.

15. R.D. Hansen, *Beyond the North-South Stalemate* (New York: McGraw-Hill, 1979), p. vii.

16. This term is derived from the number of participants at the 1968 UN Conference on Trade and Development (UNCTAD II) in New Delhi. The group now has 120 members but retains the title, sometimes shortened to G-77.

17. Jean-Jacques Servan-Schreiber, *The World Challenge* (New York: Simon and Schuster, 1981), p. 260.

18. S.B. Cohen, 'The Emergence of a New Second Order of Powers in the International System,' *Nuclear Proliferation and the Nuclear Countries*, eds. Marwah and Schulz (Cambridge: Ballinger, 1976), p. 21.

2   WHAT IS A SMALL STATE?

Scholars have been interested in small states since their rapid emergence following World War II but the subject was only accorded full treatment with the publication of Burton Benedict's *Problems of Smaller Territories*[1] in 1967. As scholarly interest increased, so did the number of different definitions of what constitutes a small state.

Some academicians favor definitions based on psychological criteria such as those advanced by R.O. Keohane, who states in part that '. . . a small power is a state whose leaders consider that it can never, acting alone or in a small group, make a significant impact on the [international] system,'[2] or Robert Rothstein, who describes a small state as: '. . . a small power . . . which recognizes that it cannot obtain security primarily by use of its own capabilities, and that it must rely fundamentally on the aid of other states, institutions, processes, or developments to do so. . .'[3]

Other observers, such as Patricia Wohlgemuth Blair[4] and J.R. Harbert,[5] emphasize population statistics in defining a small state. Blair and Harbert respectively describe a small state as a country with a population of less than 1 million. Kuznets gives a higher figure; he defines a small state as an independent sovereign state with a population of 10 million or less.[6]

Charles Taylor, on the other hand, considers the use of a single variable like population to be too narrow and subjective an approach. He uses techniques such as hierarchical clustering and analysis of variance together with criteria involving energy consumption, legal status, political self-perception, distance, population, gross national product (GNP), and land area to determine what constitutes a small state. Using cluster analysis, he constructed a statistical typology of micro and small states, combining population, GNP, and land area criteria.[7] Out of a total of 165 members in the international system (excluding the Byelorussian SSR and the Ukrainian SSR), he classifies 23 as micro-states with a population of 1 million or less, 64 as small, 63 as medium, and 13 as large.

Jean-Luc Vellut's categorization of the international system is somewhat different. He divides the states into four classes: great powers, medium powers, small powers, and smaller powers — the latter being subdivided into Class I and Class II smaller states.[8] The two major indicators used by Vellut to determine the size of states are population and gross domestic product (GDP).[9] He ranks all states first according to the size of their population and then according to their GDP. These lists are then supplemented by a logarithmic graph of the number of international bodies in which each state holds membership. Great powers are deemed to be those states in the top bracket with respect to at least three of the following indicators: population (100 million or more); GDP ($25 billion or more); special political status (veto right in the Security Council of the UN); or size of military force (300,000 or more).[10] Medium powers include '. . . states with at least one of the two main indicators (population and GDP) in the upper third of the respective logarithmic distributions, viz. a population of at least 50 million and/or a GDP of at least $10,000 million.'[11] Small powers '. . . have at least one indicator in the upper half of the scale, viz. a population of at least 10 million, and/or a GDP of $2,000 million or more.'[12] Class I smaller powers '. . . have either a population of 5 million or more, and/or a GDP of at least $1,000 million,' while Class II smaller powers fall below Class I in terms of both indicators.[13]

The United Nations also uses more than one criterion in its definition of small states: '. . . entities which are exceptionally small in area, population and human and economic resources, and which are now emerging as independent states.'[14] The emphasis, however, is placed upon the population variable, ranging from less than 1 million to 10 million.[15]

Raimo Vayrynen tackles the problem of defining a small state by identifying four possible categories into which definitions of small states can fall: definitions related to the rank of countries; definitions emphasizing the nature of the behavior of small powers; definitions based on the distinct interests of small powers as contrasted with those of great powers; and definitions applying concepts of role theory.[16] He then offers his own definition:

A small power is a state which has a low objective and/or low perceived rank in the context where it is acting. Furthermore, small powers are expected to behave in a given way, i.e., their role prescriptions differ from those of middle and great powers, which affect, together with their low rank, their behavior and possibilities of influence. Finally, the interests of small powers are at least to some extent different from the interests of great powers, a fact which denotes the latent or manifest conflict of interests between these two classes of states.[17]

Maurice East believes that the foreign policy behavior of states is an important criterion in determining their 'size,' and asserts that small states are characterized by low levels of overall participation in world affairs; high levels of activity in intergovernmental organizations (IGOs); high levels of support for international legal norms; avoidance of behavior and policies which tend to alienate the more powerful states in the system; avoidance of the use of force as a technique of statecraft; a narrow functional and geographic range of concern in foreign policy activities; and frequent utilization of moral and normative positions on international issues.[18]

The preceding discussion indicates the difficulties involved in generalizing about or even defining small states. What complicates the search for a definition is the question of which variables are the most reliable indicators of 'smallness.' As Benedict puts it, it has 'proved impossible to decide what "smallness" means with any precision. It is a comparative and not an absolute idea. Whatever scales of magnitude are employed seem arbitrary and it is difficult to pick out of them where smallness begins and ends. Countries can be small in one sense and not in another. Smallness in whatever form it may exist is only one of the variables. The issue is complicated still further by the significant factor of remoteness, whether simple geographical remoteness or remoteness from the intellectual mainstreams of the world.'[19] There are even differences of opinion over what name to assign to this group of states. Some writers refer to them as 'mini-states,' others as 'micro-states' or 'diminutive states.' In this book, they will be referred to simply as small states and defined as states with a small land area, small GNP, small population, and a low level of military capability.

Notes

1. Burton Benedict, ed. *Problems of Smaller Territories* (London: The Athlone Press, 1967). Published for the Institute of Commonwealth Studies. An earlier book by Annette Baker Fox, *The Power of Small States: Diplomacy in World War II* (Chicago: University of Chicago Press, 1959), dealt with five 'small' states and their success in remaining out of war. Though a valuable study, it was limited in scope and one could argue that the states discussed really fall into the category of medium states.

2. R.O. Keohane, 'Lilliputian's Dilemmas: Small States in International Politics,' *International Organization*, 23 (1169), p. 296. A good example of leaders' perceptions of their country are the remarks made by Zulfikar Ali Bhutto in his book, *The Myth of Independence* (London: Oxford University Press, 1969). In Chapter 2, Ali Bhutto tags Pakistan as a small nation even though it is grouped among the medium powers by most analysts.

3. R.L. Rothstein, *Alliances & Small Powers* (New York: Columbia University Press, 1968), p. 29.

4. Patricia Wohlgemuth Blair, *The Mini-State Dilemma*, Occasional Paper No. 6, Carnegie Endowment for International Peace (Oct. 1967), p. 3.

5. J.R. Harbert, 'The Behavior of the Mini-States in the United Nations, 1971-1972,' *International Organization*, 30 (1976), pp. 109-27.

6. S. Kuznets, 'Economic Growth of Small Nations,' *Economic Consequences of the Size of Nations*, ed. E.A.G. Robinson (New York: St Martin's Press, 1960), p. 28.

7. For details see Charles Taylor, 'Statistical Typology of Micro-States and Territories,' *Small States and Territories: Status and Problems*, eds. J. Rapoport, E. Muteba, and J.J. Therattil (New York: Arno Press, 1971), pp. 183-202. A UNITAR study.

8. Jean-Luc Vellut, 'Small States and the Problem of War and Peace: Some Consequences of the Emergence of Smaller States in Africa,' *Journal of Peace Research*, No. 4 (1967), p. 254.

9. *Ibid.*, p. 254.

10. *Ibid.*, p. 254.

11. *Ibid.*, p. 254.

12. *Ibid.*, p. 254.

13. *Ibid.*, p. 254.

14. UN A/6701/Add. I, 1967.

15. Kuznets, 'Economic Growth,' p. 14.

16. Raimo Vayrynen, 'On the Definition and Measurement of Small Power States,' *Cooperation and Conflict: Nordic Journal of International Politics*, 2 (1971), p. 99.

17. *Ibid.*, p. 99.

18. Maurice A. East, 'Size and Foreign Policy Behavior: A Test of Two Models,' *World Politics*, 25 (1973), p. 557.

19. Benedict, *Problems of Smaller Territories*, p. 2.

3   SMALL STATES AND THE UNITED NATIONS

While membership in the United Nations is not synonymous with participation in the international system (e.g. Switzerland), the new state phenomenon is reflected by the increase in the UN membership roster — from 45 countries at the time of the organization's establishment in 1945 to 156 in 1981 (see Table 1.2, Ch. 1). Of these, micro and small states (with a population below 5 million) number 80. The number of potential new states which might conceivably apply for UN admission in the coming decades is nearly 65 (see Table 3.1).[1] In view of the fact that almost every sovereign state today holds UN membership or is associated with the UN through one or more of its related organizations, that organization reflects the international system as it endeavors to reconcile power politics with enlightened diplomacy and international humanistic development.

Scholars and politicians are divided on what constitute appropriate UN admission criteria for a new state. Alarmed at these states' influx to the international organization, some go so far as to say that the UN itself is being jeopardized, confidence in it undermined and its capacity diminished.[2] A distinction, they say, must be made between the right of states to independence and their admission as full members to the United Nations.[3]

Some scholars argue that states with very small populations do not have the economic resources to carry out fully UN responsibilities. Early interest shown by the Vatican in joining the UN, for example, was privately discouraged by the United States on the grounds that the enclave was too small to be able to undertake such UN responsibilities as participation in UN peace forces.[4] After Liechtenstein's application was officially rejected by the League of Nations in 1920 because it was '. . . not in a position to carry out all the international obligations imposed by the covenant,'[5] the European small states of San Marino and Monaco withdrew their applications.

Some observers also claim that small states have limited human resources for adequate UN representation. For example, the members of the permanent delegation to the United Nations of the Maldives Islands (population 145,000) had to terminate their

Table 3.1: Potential Members of the International System 1981

	Islands	Sq. Miles	Population[a]	Potential Category[b]	Dependency of
WESTERN HEMISPHERE					
Anguilla	*	35	6,500	A	United Kingdom
Bermuda	*	18	57,700	A	United Kingdom
Cayman Islands	*	102	16,700	A	United Kingdom
Falkland Islands (Malvinas)	*	6,280	1,800	A	United Kingdom
Greenland	*	840,000	49,300	A	Denmark
Guadeloupe	*	658	319,000	C	France (Department)
Guiana, French		34,750	64,400	A	France (Department)
Martinique	*	417	311,900	C	France (Department)
Montserrat	*	40	11,500	A	United Kingdom
Netherlands Antilles	*	383	246,500	B	Netherlands
Puerto Rico	*	3,435	2,712,000	D	United States (Commonwealth)
St Barthelemy	*	40	2,400	A	France
St Kitts & Nevis	*	104	49,800	A	United Kingdom
St Pierre & Miquelon	*	93	5,200	A	France (Department)
Turks & Caicos	*	193	7,100	A	United Kingdom
Virgin Islands, British	*	59	13,000	A	United Kingdom
Virgin Islands, US	*	133	62,500	A	United States
EUROPE					
Azores	*	904	291,000	B	Portugal
Faeroe Islands	*	540	42,800	A	Denmark
Gibraltar	*	2	29,800	A	United Kingdom
Guernsey	*	30	54,400	A	United Kingdom
Jersey	*	45	78,000	A	United Kingdom
Man, Isle of	*	221	64,000	A	United Kingdom

	Islands	Sq. Miles	Population[a]	Potential Category[b]	Dependency of
MIDEAST AND NORTH AFRICA					
Madeira	*	307	253,000	B	Portugal
Spanish North African Presidios		14	166,000	B	Spain
SUB-SAHARAN AFRICA					
Mayotte	*	146	47,200	A	France
St Helena (with Ascension & Tristan da Cunha)	*	159	7,300	A	United Kingdom
Namibia		318,251	961,500	C	UN (South Africa)
ASIA AND INDIAN OCEAN					
Brunei	*	2,226	213,000	B	United Kingdom
Hong Kong	*	405	5,067,000	D	United Kingdom
Macao	*	6	277,300	B	Portugal
Reunion	*	970	493,300	C	France
OCEANIA					
Admirality Islands	*	800	23,000	A	Australia
American Samoa	*	77	32,400	A	United States
Austral Islands (Polynesia)	*	4,000	146,000	B	France
Bonin Islands	*	40	200	A	Japan
Caroline Islands	*	463	56,000	A	United States
Christmas Island	*	52	3,300	A	Australia
Cocos (Keeling) Islands	*	5.5	392	A	Australia
Cook Islands	*	93	21,500	A	New Zealand
Easter Island	*	64	1,000	A	Chile
Fanning Island	*	13	376	A	United Kingdom
Guam	*	212	120,000	B	United States
Johnston Atoll	*	1	1,000	A	United States
Mariana Islands	*	184	14,400	A	United States

Marquesas Islands	*	480	5,600	A	France
Marshall Islands	*	70	25,000	A	United States
Midway	*	15	2,200	A	United States
New Britain	*	14,600	166,000	B	Australia
New Caledonia	*	7,366	139,600	B	France
New Ireland	*	2,800	50,500	A	Australia
Niue Island	*	100	3,300	A	New Zealand
Norfolk Island	*	13	2,200	A	Australia
Palau (Pelew)	*	184	12,500	A	United States
Pitcairn	*	1.8	63	A	United Kingdom
Society Islands	*	150	21,000	A	France
Swain's Island	*	2	100	A	United States
Tahiti	*	402	84,500	A	France
Tokelau (Union) Islands	*	4	1,600	A	New Zealand
Tuamotu (Paumotu) Archipelago	*	330	6,700	A	France
Volcano Islands	*	8	1,200	A	Japan
Wake	*	2	2,000	A	United States
Wallis and Futuna	*	98	9,000	A	France
Washington Island	*	5	450	A	United Kingdom

Notes:
a. All population statistics are taken from the *Encyclopedia Britannica 1981 Book of the Year.*
b. Categories: (A) Micro-states (population under 100,000); (B) Micro-states (100,000–300,000); (C) Small States (300,000–1,000,000); (D) Small States (2,000,000–5,000,000).

mission for 'financial reasons'[6] and return home. Also to be taken into consideration, F. Plimpton states, are the rigors of membership, '. . . the long hours, the nervous tensions, the insolubility of many problems, the frustrations, the interminable oratory, and the exaction of the United Nations social life.'[7]

Although there is sharp disagreement on what action should be taken, almost everyone agrees that the admission of small states to the UN poses special problems. The need for establishing UN admission criteria for these states was addressed by the US representative in the Security Council on September 20, 1965 when the issue of the admission of the Maldives Islands was debated:

> Today many of the small emerging entities, however willing, probably do not have the human or economic resources at this stage to meet this second criterion (the ability to carry out UN Charter obligations). We would therefore urge that Council Members and other United Nations Members give early and careful consideration to this problem in an effort to arrive at some agreed standards — some lower limits to be applied in the case of future applicants to the UN, perhaps . . . we do not for a moment suggest the exclusion of small states from the family of nations; on the contrary, we believe we must develop for them some accommodation that will permit their close association with the UN and its broad range of activities. This is another facet of the problem that we think demands early and careful consideration.[8]

The late UN Secretary-General U Thant was another outspoken advocate of limiting UN membership. 'While universality of membership is most desirable,' he stated in a UN annual report, 'like all concepts it has to be drawn somewhere . . . it may be opportune for the competent organs to undertake a thorough and comprehensive study of the criteria for membership in the United Nations, with a view to laying down the necessary limitations on full membership.'[9] With the ever-increasing number of small states in mind, Thant observed in 1965 that:

> Their limited size and resources can pose a difficult problem as to the role they should try to play in international life. . . I believe the time has come when Member States may wish to

examine more closely the criteria for admission of new members in the light of the long-term implications of present trends.[10]

Thant was an advocate of 'observer status' for the small states, one of five options, discussed below, that have been proposed in lieu of full UN membership.

Five Possible Solutions

Observer Status. In 1965 Thant suggested that very small states be allowed to establish permanent observer missions at the UN — either in New York or in Geneva. He wrote:

> I have no doubt that the true interests of peace should be better served if non-member states were to be encouraged to maintain observers at the UN Headquarters so that they may be in a position to sense the currents and cross-currents of world opinion which are so uniquely concentrated in the Organization.[11]

A year later, he noted, '. . . it could only be of benefit to them [small states] and to the UN as a whole . . . to expose them to the impact of the work of the Organization . . . [This] would surely lead to better understanding of the world and a more realistic approach to [the solution of world problems].'[12] And in 1967, he wrote, '. . . it would be possible formally to establish the status of observer and to draw up legal rules permitting non-members to follow items of interest to them.'[13]

Observer status could prove to be the easiest solution to the small-state question and might eventually develop into a type of associate membership. Permanent observership in the General Assembly, advocates argue, would provide non-members with the opportunity to participate in Assembly debates and in various other committees. As observers, small states would not be able to vote nor would they be required to pay UN dues; expenses incurred would be for office space and a small salaried staff.

Limited Participation. This option would enable very small states to restrict their involvement in the UN to those matters that interest them and that touch upon their national interests. Limited participation would enable them to conserve manpower while giving them a voice in decisions on the few issues on the UN annual agenda affecting them. Limited participation, one of three proposals presented to the League of Nations in 1920 by a committee established to examine alternatives for small states, would enable very small states to:

> . . . enjoy all the privileges of ordinary members . . . by taking part in debates or in votes to the extent that a majority of the Assembly might decide that the national interests of these states were involved therein.[14]

Regional or Joint Membership. Regional membership means one UN membership for a grouping of states or regional organizations sharing common interests. Such an arrangement would enable small states to pool their resources and participate in more activities and committees. This option would require an amendment to the Charter, which currently permits only individual states to be full members of the UN.

Weighted Voting. One effect of the ever-increasing number of very small states in the UN is growing complaint about their voting patterns in the General Assembly. The increased size of the Assembly has diminished the voting power of the present blocs of states. In response to this trend, there have been many suggestions that the richer and larger nations be given a weighted vote; the resulting system would be similar to that now used by the World Bank and the International Monetary Fund. Such a vote would be based upon the population, industrial, and educational levels of the countries concerned as well as their capacity to contribute to UN activities.

UN Services and Technical Assistance. The fifth option proposed for small states in lieu of full UN membership is the provision to them of UN technical services and assistance. Advocates of this option feel that the UN — because of its part in dismantling colonial empires — has a moral obligation to make good its promise to 'render all help to peoples of those territories in their efforts to decide their future status.'[15] Rapoport asserts that such help must be provided to the small states and that a commitment to do so is implicit in the 'Declaration on the Granting of Independence to Colonial Countries and Peoples,' or the 'Gospel of Decolonization' as he calls it. The first three paragraphs of this Declaration (also found in Ch. 1) are important enough to be repeated here:

1. The subjection of peoples to alien subjugation, domination and exploitation constitutes a denial of fundamental human rights, is contrary to the Charter of the United Nations and is an impediment to the promotion of world peace and cooperation.
2. All peoples have the right to self-determination; by virtue of that right, they freely determine their political status and freely pursue their economic, social and cultural development.
3. Inadequacy of political, economic, social or educational preparedness should never serve as a pretext for delaying independence.[16]

Rapoport comments as follows:

Self-determination must be exercised without strings attached: at the time people choose their new status, their choice must be unrestricted; and they may choose independence if they prefer, however small and poor their territory may be . . . The two major concerns of the United Nations are that the choice should be free; and that the choice should be informed.[17]

Fisher believes that a special office to facilitate the granting of UN assistance to the ministates should be established within the UN. He suggests a possible scenario for the compartmentalization of such assistance:

. . . The easy part, as I have suggested, is providing assistance of a technical or economic nature. . . It could be improved, I surmise, if small places could look to a single office which would know about both national and international programs for which they might qualify.

The more difficult problem relates to political and legal advice. A small state needs advice about its constitution and about relationships with larger states. For the small states that are 'wholly independent,' one can readily conceive of a UN advisory service which included such legal and political advice.[18]

The above suggests there is no consensus on what form UN assistance should take, especially for newly emerging states:

> The UN role with respect to a dependent territory, needless to say, is well defined, whereas after decolonization, it is not so clear. Both the Charter as well as the practice of the UN, as expressed notably in the Declaration on the Granting of Independence to Colonial Countries and Peoples, Resolution 1514 (XV), provide the framework for UN authority and powers before decolonization. However, neither Article 4 of the Charter nor the practice of the United Nations offers such clear and helpful guidelines on what the UN could or should do in the case of a territory which emerges as a sovereign entity.[19]

Toward Universality

Despite the various caveats discussed earlier in this chapter, membership in the UN is very attractive to small states. Through it, they achieve a status of equality in an international setting, widen their contacts, improve their security (because of UN help in restraining bigger powers), and receive development assistance. The desire of small states for security is so large a consideration, in fact, that it prompted the late UN Secretary-General Dag Hammarskjöld to write, 'It is not . . . big powers which need the UN for their protection, it is all the others.'[20] *The Economist*, commenting on Kuwait's independence and acceptance as a full member in the UN in 1961, states that, 'Certainly Kuwait has built up a surer defense by getting itself accepted as an independent state — or anyhow a fair imitation of one, than by depending on the protection of British troops.'[21]

While historically the international system has been dominated by the 'great powers,' today it is less so, and the United Nations reflects this change. With increasing diffusions of power among states, smaller states now have greater leverage than ever before in the UN and use such techniques as solidarity grouping within the UN (including voting with the nonaligned bloc) and regional bloc voting. Contrary to the claims of some observers, small states generally vote to protect their own national interests; they do not ape the 'great powers.' In a study of the UN voting behavior of small states, J.R. Harbert comments:

1. There is greatest ministate cohesion on colonial and economic issues and less cohesion on social, humanitarian, and cultural questions. Political issues divide the ministates.
2. The ministates and the USSR vote similarly on colonial and economic questions, whereas the ministates' voting is more similar to that of the US and the colonial powers on social, humanitarian, and cultural issues. On political issues, the ministates are neither a bloc nor the subservient clients of the superpowers.
3. With few exceptions, ministates' voting patterns are similar to those of the African-Asian group in the UN.[22]

Harbert concludes that:

One can argue reasonably that most ministates have behaved rather 'responsibly' in the UN. Although their delegations and missions tend to be significantly smaller than average, the ministates have participated on a regular, if necessarily limited, basis in Assembly affairs. More important, despite their economic and strategic weakness, the ministates do not appear to have been susceptible to 'arm-twisting or vote buying' by larger states on political issues. Indeed their interests seem to coincide with what we know to be the concerns of the other 'new' nations in the UN.[23]

The current trend in the UN, then, is to accept for membership states, regardless of size, that fall within the general guidelines of Article 4(1) of the UN Charter:

Membership in the UN is open to all other peace-loving states which accept the obligations in the present Charter and, in the judgement of the Organization, are able and willing to carry out these obligations.

The International Court of Justice has determined that five specific criteria for UN membership are included in the above Article. They are: be a state, be peace-loving, accept the obligations of the

Charter, be able to carry out those obligations, and be willing to do so.[24] Article 4(2) of the Charter places responsibility for approval of a state's membership application on the General Assembly, upon the recommendation of the Security Council.

Although the increasing number of very small states in the UN has contributed to the decline of Western power in the General Assembly, this decline is not destructive to the international system and is not a good reason to limit the membership of the United Nations. Some object that such potential applicants for membership as Turks and Caicos (population 7,100) should not have the same voting rights as other states since they could not provide commensurate services. Farran has an answer to that:

> While it may be argued that it is contrary to 'justice' to give San Marino the same vote as Italy, it may be as contrary to 'justice' if the population of the diminutive states are the only human beings in the world unrepresented in the Assembly . . . A legal system is indeed crude . . . if it only does justice among the middle class of its community.[25]

If the United Nations, which helped in the process of decolonization, should now consider imposing restrictions upon the memberships of very small states, it would be faced with a serious contradiction. If such a step were taken, the UN would become a Club for the Privileged and would dishonor its original concept of universality. Even the possible enlargement of the General Assembly to 200 members or more would, in the opinion of this writer, be a healthy development. Such an enlargement would enhance world peace through increased international contacts and understanding and through a lessening of tension among the larger powers. Whatever solution is decided upon — observer status, limited participation, regional membership, weighted voting, or technical assistance — the UN must devise a workable formula for the establishment of admission criteria for small states with limited resources.

Notes

1. The United Nations recognizes three ways in which a non-self-governing territory can attain self-government: emergence as a sovereign independent state, free association with an independent state, and integration with another state.
2. U. Whitaker, 'Mini-Membership for Mini-States,' *War–Peace Report*, Vol. 7, No. 3 (Apr. 1967), p. 3.
3. General Assembly Official Records (GAOR): 22nd session, 1966, Suppl. No. 1A (A/6701/Add., I.).
4. C. Hull, *The Memoirs of Cordell Hull* (New York: Macmillan, 1948), Vol. II, pp. 1711-12.
5. League of Nations, *Records*, First Assembly, p. 667.
6. The United Kingdom has been covering some of the costs of membership of the Maldives.
7. F.T.O. Plimpton, 'The United Nations Needs Family Planning,' *New York Times Magazine*, September 18, 1966, p. 97.
8. Doc. S/PV. 1243, p. 31.
9. GAOR, 22nd Session, 1967, Suppl. No. 1A, para. 162 and 165.
10. GAOR, 20th Session, 1965, Suppl. No. 1A, p. 2.
11. GAOR, 20th Session, 1965, Suppl. No. 1A, p. 11.
12. GAOR, 21st Session, 1966, Suppl. No. 1A, p. 14.
13. UN, *Annual Report of the Secretary-General*, 1967.
14. League of Nations, *Records*, Second Assembly, pp. 686-8.
15. GA Res. 2232, 21 UN GAOR, Suppl. 10-16, at 74, UN Doc. A/6316 (1966).
16. J.G. Rapoport, 'The Participation of Ministates in International Affairs,' *Proceedings, American Society of International Law* (1968), p. 156.
17. *Ibid.*, p. 157.
18. R. Fisher, 'The Participation of Ministates in International Affairs,' *American Society of International Law* (1968), p. 168. Also see, United Nations Doc. A/AC, 109/SC, 85-7, August 28-30, 1967.
19. M.S. Esfandiary, former Iranian representative to the UN and Rapporteur of the Committee of 24; see *Proceedings, American Society of International Law* (1968), p. 171.
20. GAOR, 15th Session, 883rd Plenary Session, October 3, 1960.
21. *The Economist*, May 21, 1966, p. 803.
22. J.R. Harbert, 'The Behavior of the Mini-states in the United Nations, 1971-1972,' *International Organization*, 30 (Winter 1976), p. 109.
23. *Ibid.*, p. 127.
24. International Court of Justice, *Reports*, 1948 Advisory Opinion, p. 62.
25. C. d'Olivier Farran, 'The Position of Diminutive States in International Law,' in *Internationalrechtliche und Staatsrechtliche Abhandlungen* (Hermes, Dusseldorf, 1960), p. 145.

4 THE ECONOMIES, FOREIGN POLICIES, AND SECURITY OF SMALL STATES, WITH EXAMPLES FROM THE GULF

Economy

The economies of states with small areas and populations, i.e. small states, are vulnerable and highly sensitive to external changes. The oil-producing countries of the Gulf, for example, are heavily dependent upon such uncontrollable external factors as the fluctuating foreign markets for almost all their imports and for the oil they sell abroad. In much of what follows we will focus on Kuwait, Qatar, and the UAE (the three most significant oil producers among the small Arab states of the Gulf) and Saudi Arabia (technically a medium power, but one sharing many of the vulnerabilities of the Gulf's smaller states). We will refer to these four countries collectively as the 'Gulf four.'

Although the market for oil has traditionally been strong and seems likely to remain so for the foreseeable future, there are nevertheless risks associated with heavy reliance on a single natural resource for national income, export receipts, and budgetary revenues. In Table 4.1 the high degree of reliance on oil exports by the Gulf four is illustrated by the ratio of oil revenues to GDP, which ranges from 60.3 percent for the UAE to 73.8 percent for Qatar; by the ratio of oil receipts to total export receipts, which ranges from 87.7 percent to 99.7 percent; and by the ratio of oil revenues to total budget receipts, which ranges from 83.1 percent to 92 percent. These ratios clearly show that if the oil sector were to experience some disruption, politically motivated or otherwise, these countries would have no economic base on which to draw for economic growth or for meeting their budgetary and balance of payments needs. The vulnerability of these countries is further illustrated in the statistics on exports, imports, and oil prices given in Table 4.2. As can be seen from these data, the value of imports in US dollars in 1980 was nearly 20 times the 1972 figure. This growth in imports was sustained only by the rapid rise in export receipts, made possible by the rising price of oil and an increasing volume of oil exports. Figure 4.1 shows that oil export receipts

Table 4.1: The Gulf Four: Measures of Dependence on Oil (Average for the three years ending in 1980: in percent)

	Oil Revenues/ GDP	Oil Receipts/ Total Exports	Oil Revenues/ Total Budget Receipts
Saudi Arabia	64.5	99.7	88.4
Kuwait	64.9	92.7	83.1
U.A.E.	60.3	87.7	89.4
Qatar	73.8	96.0	92.0

Sources: International Monetary Fund, *International Financial Statistics*, various issues, and official sources.

Table 4.2: The Gulf Four: Exports, Imports, and Average Oil Export Price

	Exports	Imports	Average Oil Export Price (US $ per barrel)
	(In millions of US dollars)		
1972	8,595.7	2,555	2.40
1973	13,493.8	4,044	5.46
1974	49,974.7	6,388	9.85
1975	45,419.0	9,686	11.06
1976	57,174.1	16,163	11.63
1977	62,639.8	25,770	12.63
1978	59,862.4	31,566	15.47
1979	93,289.1	37,830	20.08
1980	148,211.6	44,799	30.47

Source: IMF, *International Financial Statistics* (lines 70..d and 71..d), and staff estimates.

varied in a jagged fashion during 1972-80, whereas imports rose steadily. Figure 4.2 displays changes in oil export receipts, import payments, and the average export price of oil relative to a 1972 base. This chart further highlights the variability of exports as opposed to the persistent increase in import payments. This variability is clearly a reflection, at least in part, of the variability in the export price of oil.

The economic vulnerability discussed above has led to significant fluctuations in the per capita income of the populations in the Gulf region. This income is directly related to the prices and amounts of oil exports, which in turn are dependent upon external conditions. For example, it appears that the real average per capita income in Kuwait declined by 2.5 percent annually between 1950 and 1975. An estimated $19,000 in the early 1950s (in terms of 1974 currency values), the average per capita income had dropped to $10,000 in 1975.

Thus, while the Gulf four are often cited as 'rich' countries with high per capita incomes, the concept of per capita income is not entirely appropriate with regard to these countries. In the first place, the value added in the oil sector, which, as indicated above, provides the bulk of total GDP, does not reflect the process of income generation in the traditional sense. It merely represents the exchange of one asset, the exhaustible oil resource, for another, financial assets. In order to measure per capita income in these countries one needs to adjust for the distorting presence of the oil sector. In Table 4.3 the non-oil GDP of the four Gulf countries is indicated together with the per capita GDP adjusted for the effect of the oil sector. Even these figures, which range from just over $5,000 per capita to nearly $14,000, exaggerate the

Figure 4.1: The Gulf Four: Oil Export Receipts and Import Payments, 1972-80 (In billions of US dollars)

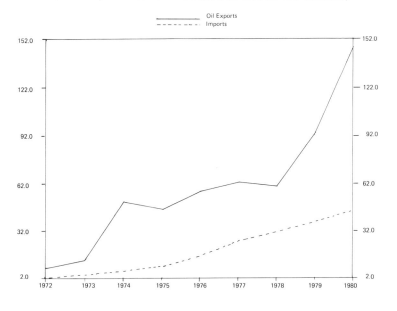

Figure 4.2: The Gulf Four: Indices of Exports, Imports and
the Average Export Price of Crude Oil 1972-80 (1972 = 100)

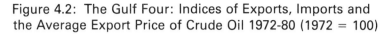

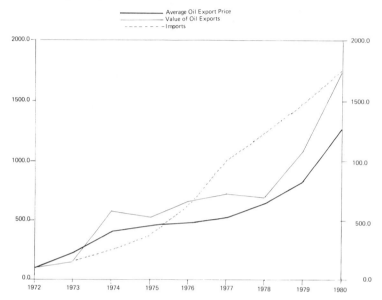

true level of production in these countries, since much of the
economic activity in the non-oil sectors is directly or indirectly
attributable to oil sector operations.

In Table 4.4, per capita GDP for Kuwait is calculated (without
the adjustment for the effects of the oil sector) for the period 1962-
79 (see also Figs. 4.4 and 4.5). The data indicate that although
nominal income in Kuwait has risen considerably during that
period, the real per capita GDP, after adjustment for inflation, has
hardly risen at all. The real per capita GDP of Kuwait appears to
have declined almost uninterruptedly from 1962 until 1973; it
jumped in 1974 as a result of the oil price increases of that year but
then mostly declined again through 1978 before jumping up once
more in 1979 (as a result of oil price increases in that year). On the
whole, for the period 1962-79 the annual average increase in
nominal GDP on a per capita basis was 7.7 percent, but the
corresponding figure for real per capita GDP was only 0.6 percent.
These results reflect the unstable nature of economic development
in the Gulf four and point to an inherent structural problem in
these countries.

The 1981 oil glut, precipitated by Saudi oil policy, highlights the vulnerability of the economies of the small Gulf states. The continuation of the glut could have adverse effects upon the economies of the OPEC countries, especially those of the Gulf. The values of Arab and Nigerian light-grade oils declined by $7.30 per barrel between January and June 1981 (see Fig. 4.3). Nigerian production reportedly fell below 900,000 barrels a day, or less than 50 percent of this country's 2 million barrel a day capacity.

The government of a small state often represents the largest economic sector in the country, performing tasks that are normally carried out by other sectors in larger states and operating enterprises that may be unattractive to private individuals or organizations because of the financial risks involved. This holds true for the main Arab oil exporting states of the Gulf, where the governments' monopoly of the oil sector and their desire to distribute wealth to achieve political stability have caused these countries to take on some welfare-state characteristics.[1] For example, Table 4.5 illustrates the extensive participation of Kuwait's government in national private and semi-private shareholding companies established between 1952 and 1977.

It is widely believed that the existence of vast oil reserves in a country means that its economic development is inevitable. This is not necessarily true.[2] If a country fails to utilize its limited natural resources through well-organized social institutions, the twin goals of economic development and economic independence may never be realized. As S. Kuznets points out:

. . . the existence of valuable natural resources represents a permissive condition and facilitates — if properly exploited — the transition from pre-industrial to industrial phases of growth. But unless the nation shows a capacity for modifying its social institutions in time to take advantage of the opportunity, it will have only a transient effect. Advantages in natural resources never last too long — given continuous changes in technology and its extension to other parts of the world . . . To put it differently: every small nation has some advantage in natural resources — whether it be location, coastline, minerals, forests, etc . . . But some show a capacity to build on it, if only as a starting point towards a process of sustained economic growth, and others do not. The crucial variables are elsewhere, and they must be sought in the nation's social and economic institutions.[3]

Table 4.3: The Gulf Four: GDP and Per Capita GDP, 1980

	GDP (US$ billion)	Non-oil GDP (US$ billion)	Population (million)	Per Capita Non-oil GDP (US$)
Saudi Arabia	144.3	43.9	8.37	5,250
Kuwait	27.3	8.2	1.36	6,030
UAE	30.0	11.0	0.797	13,790
Qatar	6.8	1.3	0.216	5,875

Sources: International Monetary Fund, *International Financial Statistics*, various issues, and official sources.

Figure 4.3: Crude Pricing, by Fiat and Market

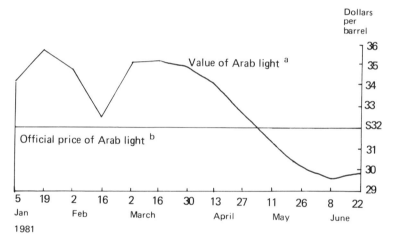

Notes: a. Compared from spot prices in Rotterdam. b. Set in December, 1980.
Source: Platt's Oil Price Service.

Professor Kuznets cites the historical example of Brazil, which in the nineteenth century '. . . enjoyed several times the position of a supplier of natural resources in world-wide demand; yet the record of this country's economic growth has not been impressive, and it is not as yet among the economically advanced nations.'[4]

Because of their reliance upon foreign experts and skills, the Gulf four are not able to achieve economic independence. Although a self-sustaining reservoir of skilled manpower could in principle be developed through education in general and higher

Table 4.4: Kuwait: Per Capita GDP (In US dollars)

	Nominal	% Δ	Real[a]	% Δ
1962	5,224		11,721	
1963	4,875	− 6.7	10,764	− 8.2
1964	4,819	− 1.2	10,493	− 2.5
1965	4,427	− 8.1	9,492	− 9.4
1966	4,598	3.9	9,620	1.4
1967	4,284	− 6.8	8,933	− 7.1
1968	4,295	0.3	9,019	1.0
1969	4,072	− 5.2	8,272	− 8.3
1970	3,882	− 4.7	7,524	− 9.0
1971	4,919	26.7	9,043	20.2
1972	5,298	7.7	8,882	− 1.8
1973	6,109	15.3	8,497	− 4.3
1974	13,834	126.4	15,412	81.4
1975	12,017	− 13.1	12,017	− 22.0
1976	12,391	3.1	12,323	2.5
1977	12,517	1.0	11,533	− 6.4
1978	12,708	1.5	10,371	− 10.1
1979	18,355	44.4	12,932	24.7

Note: a. Deflated by industrial countries' export unit price index (weighted average of the countries' exports).
Source: IMF, *IFS*, October 1981.

education in particular, at present, social, political, and economic factors render education largely ineffectual as a source of much-needed indigenous skills and expertise.[5] Furthermore, the increase in capital funds following the rise in oil prices and production has had an adverse impact upon the people of the Gulf in terms of their motivation for hard work and their efforts toward building the basis of an economy independent of oil revenues. Riad El-Sheikh sums up the situation as follows:

. . . the abundance of capital funds does not necessarily lead to the abundance of other factors which are prerequisites for economic growth. It can pay for capital goods, but not necessarily for their full utilization. In addition, it may weaken the effort-reward relationship and with it the will to economize and to develop. Thus, in the main, the conditions on the side of factor supplies — widely defined to include attitudes to work and favorable social motivation system — tend to remain exhibiting a state of imbalance.[6]

Figure 4.4: Kuwait Per Capita GDP in Nominal and in
Real Terms, 1962-79 (In thousands of US dollars)

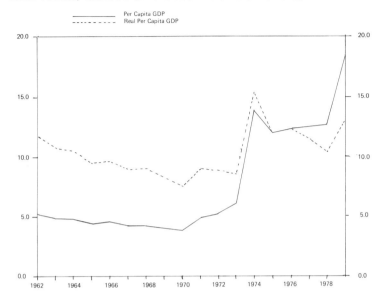

Figure 4.5: Kuwait Indices of Nominal and Real
Per Capita GDP, 1962-79

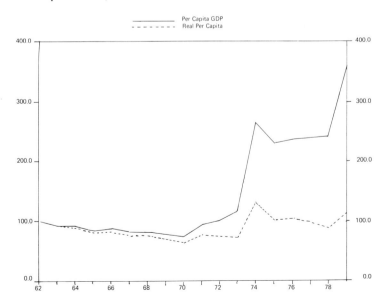

Table 4.5: The Development of Private and Semi-Private Kuwaiti Share-holding Companies, 1952-77

Name of Company	Date of Establishment	Authorized Capital (KD million)	Government Participation (%)
National Bank of Kuwait	29.05.52	13,612,500	1
Kuwait Cinema Company	05.10.54	1,635,263	49
Kuwait Oil Tankers Company	19.09.57	25,936,605	
Commercial Bank	15.06.60	14,440,000	
Kuwait Insurance Company	10.08.60	2,333,325	1.6
Gulf Bank	29.10.60	7,044,465	
National Industries Company	08.12.60	6,300,000	51
Kuwait Flour Mills Company	25.10.61	2,000,000	100
Kuwait Investment Company	03.12.61	11,269,130	50
Gulf Insurance Company	07.04.62	2,560,000	67.6
Al-Ahliya Insurance Company	30.04.62	1,690,000	5
Kuwait Hotels Company	25.06.62	2,941,180	49
Kuwait Transport Company	15.09.62	4,000,000	74.7
Kuwait Foodstuffs Company	23.11.63	1,320,000	
Kuwait Foreign Trading and Contracting Company	26.12.64	25,000,000	82.4
Metal Pipe Industries Company	19.06.66	4,800,000	1.2
Al-Ahli Bank	17.06.67	7,000,000	
Kuwait Cement Company	23.10.68	6,500,000	28
Kuwait United Fisheries Co.	18.01.71	10,000,000	48.2
Bank of Kuwait and the Middle East	27.11.71	8,000,000	49
Kuwait Real Estate Company	09.05.72	10,000,000	4.8
Refrigeration and Cold Storage Co.	15.02.73	4,000,000	27.2
United Real Estate	22.03.73	15,000,000	42.8
Real Estate Bank of Kuwait	06.05.73	7,558,680	
National Real Estate Company	24.06.73	12,600,000	78.1
National Automotive Manuf. and Trading Company	10.07.73	3,600,000	61.7

Kuwait International Investment	13.09.73	12,030,000	7.9
Livestock Transport and Trade	24.11.73	9,968,176	30.4
Shipbuilding and Repair Company	30.03.74	10,000,000	100
Kuwait United Poultry Company	30.11.74	4,000,000	33.7
Gulf Cables Company	15.03.75	3,000,000	33.7
Sanitary Ware Industries	21.05.75	6,750,000	35
Burgan Bank	24.12.75	10,000,000	51
Melamine Industries	25.04.76	4,000,000	
Agricultural Food Products	26.05.76	10,000,000	
United Arab Navigation Company	01.07.76	34,800,000	66.8
Warbah Insurance Company	24.10.76	4,000,000	51
Kuwait Tire Company	28.11.76	8,000,000	
Kuwait Finance House	23.03.77	10,000,000	49
Overland Transport Company	06.07.77	10,000,000	
		346,689,324	

Source: Al-Ahli Bank, 1981.

The temptation to waste capital surplus is indeed characteristic of human nature, but small states might well follow the example of Norway, a small state rich in oil, which has limited its oil production to no more than 10 percent of its GNP.[7] It is also worth noting that the legislature of the oil-rich US state of Alaska recently convened in special session to discuss the governor's proposal that the state constitution be revised to limit what many considered runaway spending of the state's oil revenues. Like many OPEC decision-makers, the governor believed that a spending limitation is crucial to protect the state against bankruptcy when the oil runs dry. Alaska's reaction to its oil wealth has resembled that of some OPEC states; during 1979-80, it spent more money than it did during the 20 years after it became a state in 1959.[8]

Foreign Policy

In general, the theories of social science are based on the past experience of the Western world. In particular, the field of comparative foreign policy utilizes such Western-oriented theories. Christopher Hill notes that foreign policy theorists concerned with the Third World and small states have been inclined to use one of the following three approaches: (1) apply to small states a preexisting model developed from studies of already-modernized countries; (2) develop a special frame of reference that focuses exclusively on the behavior of young states with little experience or influence in international politics; or (3) combine the first two approaches.[9] Such methods are ineffective. They can lead to grave mistakes on the part of Western powers interested in the foreign policy of small states because they do not sufficiently take into consideration the cultural, historical, and socio-economic uniqueness of the developing world.

For example, the process of nationalism that gave rise to the modern European state-system differs greatly from that of the small developing state. Professor Jacob Ajayi states that

. . . in contrast to 19th century Europe where the basic aim of nationalism was to fit people who shared the same culture and language into a nation state, the fundamental yearning of African nationalism has been to weld peoples speaking different languages and having different cultures into one nation state.[10]

Rupert Emerson argues that one of the paradoxes of nationalism is that its very success in binding men together has as its counterpart '. . . its intensification of their sense of separation from those on the other side.'[11] If in the European case this sense of separation has existed between various nations, in the majority of developing countries it is present within the nation itself. Indeed, few of the newly emerged states, if any, have achieved political integration. Civil war and/or communal and ethnic divisions are part of the scene in recently independent states.

To understand the foreign policy of small states, one has to understand the psychology of their leaders and decision-makers, many of whom have experienced colonial rule firsthand. Richard Snyder and his associates argue that since political action is undertaken by concrete and identifiable human beings, the way to understand the dynamics of this action is to find out how these human actors view the world. To do this, they say, the analyst should examine their behavior in order to determine how the leaders choose one course of action from among a number of competing alternatives. It is this act of choice which is held to constitute a decision.[12]

Important decisions in small states are particularly likely to evolve from personality more than system. In his book, *The Hero and the Crowd in the Colonial Polity*, A.W. Singham states that the political processes of very small communities are characterized by a highly personalized form of government and an authoritarian form of decision-making. In a situation of personal government, one individual may be predominantly influential in choosing government policies and may often assume complete responsibility for the execution of these policies as well. Such a situation stands in contrast to that of a representative government in which the enunciation and execution of policies is basically the result of a process of interaction between cooperating and competing elites.[13] While a personalized political system may nominally be a representative form of government, it is usually a one-man show when it comes to decision-making and policy enunciation. Cabinet members are obliged to consult the leader even in very trivial matters related to their ministries. The result is an overwhelmed leader, busy with day-to-day decision-making at every government level, with no time left for future planning and reflection. Oxaal sums it up by saying:

The traditional recruitment process to political organization in very small states can be highly informal. Such a process of recruitment often stresses personal acquaintance and character endorsement by those already in the group. This means in effect, that the attainment and maintenance of leadership position proceeds along a network of personal relationship. Loyalty to the leadership, a conformity within the structure, is given a greater emphasis than competitiveness and innovation. These factors are a source of support for the predominant role of the leader in the microstate decision-making process.[14]

The size and sophistication of a state's population also influences foreign policy. This is especially true in the small, 'underdeveloped' state where foreign policy options are severely curtailed. Foreign ministries are usually understaffed, there are a relatively small number of embassies abroad, information sources are usually limited and frequently controlled or dominated by foreign interests, and there are few indigenous experts to call upon when problems arise.[15] The Grand Duchy of Luxembourg, for example, has only 10 diplomatic emissaries, accredited to 10 states, and relies on a neighbor to represent it to more than 50 other governments. One small state accredits a single ambassador to more than 10 African states, while another has 9 ambassadors covering more than 40 countries. In the 1940s and 1950s, Yemen had one ambassador representing it to the whole world. A large population, on the other hand, can enhance foreign policy capabilities, industrial strength, and military power. It can have a significant impact upon the country's international activities even if the country is poor in material terms. This is why India plays a major role in the activities of the international system, and why Egypt, although one of the poorest countries in the Arab world, plays a significant role in Arab and international politics.[16] Whether the population is large or small, its social, cultural, and political characteristics can play an influential role in determining foreign policy. The challenge confronting small states, then, is to increase the cohesiveness and sense of community of their populations and to provide for more direct interaction between the governors and the governed.

Foreign policy is also determined by and dependent upon communication and information retrieval networks. 'Great' powers certainly appreciate the adage 'knowledge is power'; in 1964, for example, the British Foreign Office spent 2 million pounds (7 percent of its total budget) on communications alone.[17] K. Deutsh[18] and David Vital reached similar conclusions on the importance of a state's capability for intelligence gathering, and observed that the 'great' powers' knowledge of a given small state's own region is often more extensive than that of the small state itself; and that the 'great' powers have the advantage of a world-wide intelligence network and are usually better able to anticipate the moves of the smaller power than the latter is capable of predicting theirs.[19]

Some observers believe that foreign policy in small states is recruited to the state-building task. Robert Good, for example, describes foreign policy as serving four purposes: continuing the revolution against colonial rule, establishing the identity of the new state, keeping an in-group in power, and reducing foreign influence at home.[20] Yet, on the whole, the foreign policies of small states are reactive to events within the international system. Not surprisingly, immediate security and survival are the highest priority (this subject is treated separately in the following section). There is little, if any, long-term or contingency planning to meet future crisis situations. Holsti observes that 'one often looks in vain for the "foreign policy" of many of the microstates; these little entities appear to be more objects than actors in the system.'[21]

Security and Survival

Shall I join with other nations in alliance?
if allies are weak, am I not best alone?
if allies are strong with power to protect me
might they not protect me out of all I own?[22]

The puzzlement so apparent in these lines is not imaginary. It is a concern of the leaders of many small states, including those in the Gulf. They are aware of the danger so clearly stated by V.V. Sveics: '. . . that a great power or any other state having disproportionate military strength may act to deprive in whole or in part a small nation of its physical existence, national identity, or independence.'[23] Even if such a direct threat is averted by international pressures, intervention in some form is still a real danger; indeed, Singer argues that outside intervention in the affairs of weak countries is inevitable and almost intrinsic to international relations.[24] A small state, as Vital puts it, '. . . is more vulnerable to pressure, more likely to give way under stress, more limited in respect of the political options open to it and subject to a tighter connection between domestic and external affairs.'[25] Throughout history, such states have been forced to seek protection from a more powerful state, which might in turn deprive the protectorate of its basic right of self-determination and independence. (Such a role was played by Britain in the Gulf region for more than a century.) In Vital's words,

> . . . the smaller the human and material resources of a state, the greater are the difficulties it surmounts if it is to maintain any valid political options at all . . . in consequence, the smaller the state, the less viable it is as a genuinely independent member of the international community.[26]

In their desperate search for survival, small states have sometimes tried to maintain their freedom by proclaiming their neutrality with respect to the great-power struggles of their day. But the fate of Belgium and the Netherlands in World War II shows that neutrality works only so long as more powerful neighbors are willing to respect it and are not interested in seizing what the neutral state has to offer. Annette Baker Fox concludes in her study, *The Power of Small States*:

> . . . [a] small state's 'benevolent neutrality' toward the dominant side during the war, indicates that the decisions of small states are likely to increase the imbalance between two power constellations. Instead of moving toward the side of the less powerful and thereby helping to restore the balance, they tend to comply with the demands of the more powerful and thus to accentuate any shifts in the balance of forces caused by changing fortunes of war or prospects of ultimate victory. Viewed in this way, the small state's characteristic behavior may be described as 'anti-balance of power' while that of a great power is characteristically 'pro-balance of power.' Where the margin between a self-righting balance and the complete overturn of the balance is very close, this behavior pattern may conceivably be decisive.[27]

R.L. Rothstein concurs with Fox in this analysis and arrived at similar conclusions.[28]

The security and survival of beleaguered small states like those in the Gulf lie not in alliance or other forms of semi-permanent association with more powerful states but in the establishment of a community composed of all those states in a region which seek security against both internal and external threats. (The Gulf Cooperation Council, discussed in Ch. 6, may become the basis for one such community.) As Van Wagenen describes it, such an organization would be '. . . a group which has become integrated, where integration is defined as the attainment of a sense of community, accompanied by formal or informal institutions and practices, sufficiently strong and widespread to assure peaceful change among members of a group with "reasonable" certainty over a "long" period of time.'[29]

Karl Deutsch suggests that such a community could be formed through political amalgamation, or

> . . . the merging of several political units or enforcement agencies into one. Such amalgamation might be the result of the voluntary merging of several previously independent provinces or countries into a single unitary state. Alternatively, it might be achieved by establishing a federal union with a federal army or police forces superior in power to those of its constituent units, and at the same time immune to the danger of becoming divided internally. Or it might be created by subjecting several previously sovereign states or federations to a common government having its own superior armed forces whose unity rested on their bonds of loyalty to it and to each other. In short, such amalgamation of smaller units into larger ones could be accomplished in many ways—by conquest, by explicit agreement, by gradual habituation, or by various combinations of these.

It could also be secured by efforts to bring about:

> . . . an increasing acceptance and use of the same or equivalent patterns of living, thinking, and feeling among individuals who are members of the various political units that are to make up the security community, so as to produce either a common 'we feeling' among them or a devotion of most of them to some symbols representing this security community or shared image of its population.[30]

The foreign policy of such a security community must be based on neutrality and its top priority must be to convince any power pressuring it that its continued neutrality is also advantageous to that power. Here, the most important tool is diplomacy — indeed, excellence in diplomacy is essential to the survival of such a community. Since the community cannot hope to win an armed struggle with external foes, it must avoid the use of force as a tool of statecraft and must rely instead upon international legal norms and negotiation; behavior· that would seriously anger more powerful states must be eschewed.

Notes

1. I. Svennilson, 'The Concept of the Nation and its Relevance to Economic Analysis,' *Economic Consequences of the Size of Nations*, ed. E.A.G. Robinson (New York: St Martin's Press, 1960), p. 5.

2. R. El-Sheikh, *Kuwait: Economic Growth of the Oil States, Problems and Policies* (Kuwait: University of Kuwait Press, 1972), p. 8.

3. S. Kuznets, 'Economic Growth of Small Nations,' *Economic Consequences of the Size of Nations*, ed. E.A.G. Robinson (New York: St Martin's Press, 1960)

4. Ibid., p. 28.

5. For a brief and precise description of the problems of higher education in the Gulf area, see H.A. Al-Ebraheem and R.P. Stevens, 'Organization, Management and Academic Problems in the Arab University: The Kuwait University Experience,' *Higher Education*, 9 (1980), pp. 203-18.

6. El-Sheikh, *Kuwait*, pp. 8-9. Also, for details on this topic, see Y. Sayegh, *The Economies of the Arab World: Development since 1945* (New York: St Martin's Press, 1978).

7. The situation in the Arab oil countries is, of course, different than in Norway. Odeh Oburdene, 'The Investment Income of Saudi Arabia and Kuwait,' (unpublished, June 1981) summarizes the situation of these countries as far as their oil production is concerned by saying, 'It is clear that there would be no surplus funds at all if oil production in these countries is a function of their economic needs. To do this, of course, would not only spell ruin for the advanced countries and, consequently to Saudi Arabia and Kuwait, but might even lead to the seizure of their foreign assets as well as their oil fields.'

8. *Washington Post*, July 14, 1981, p. A-3.

9. Christopher Hill, 'Theories of Foreign Policy Making for the Developing Countries,' *Foreign Policy Making in Developing States*, ed. Christopher Clapham (London: Saxon House, 1977), pp. 1-11.

10. J.F.A. Ajayi, 'The Place of African History and Culture in the Process of Nation-Building in Africa South of the Sahara,' *Journal of Negro Education*, 30 (1961), p. 202.

11. R. Emerson, *From Empire to Nation* (Cambridge: Harvard University Press, 1960), p. 329.

12. For details, see R.C. Snyder, H.W. Bruck, and B. Spain, *Decision-Making as an Approach to the Study of International Politics* (Princeton: Princeton University Press, 1954), Foreign Policy Analysis, Series 3.

13. A.W. Singham, *The Hero and the Crowd in the Colonial Polity* (New Haven: Yale University Press, 1967), p. 323.

14. I. Oxaal, *Black Intellectuals Come to Power* (Cambridge, Massachusetts: Schenkman, 1967), p. 142.

15. For details, see M.A. East, 'Foreign Policy Making in Small States: Some Theoretic Observations Based on the Study of Uganda's Foreign Ministry,' *Policy Science*, 4 (Dec. 1973), pp. 491-508; and Marvin C. Ott, 'Foreign Policy Formulation in Malaysia,' *Asian Survey*, 12 (1972), pp. 225-91.

16. For a fascinating and detailed study of the role played by Egypt in the Arab world since the early 1950s, see A.I. Dawisha, *Egypt in the Arab World* (New York: John Wiley and Sons, 1976). The Egyptian population constitutes more than 30 percent of the total population of the Arab world.

17. David Vital, *The Inequality of States: A Study of the Small Power in International Relations* (Oxford: Clarendon Press, 1967), p. 26.

18. K.W. Deutsch, *The Nerves of Government* (New York: Free Press, 1963).

19. Vital, *The Inequality of States*, pp. 22-3.

20. Robert Good, 'State-Building as Determinant of Foreign Policy in the New States,' *Neutralism and Non-Alignment: The New States in World Affairs*, ed. L. Martin (New York: Praeger, 1962), pp. 3-12.

21. K.J. Holsti, 'Retreat from Utopia: International Relations Theory, 1945-1970,' *Canadian Journal of Political Science*, 4 (1971), p. 174.

22. Richard Rodgers and Oscar Hammerstein 2nd, 'A Puzzlement,' *The King and I*, Copyright (c) 1951 by Williamson Music, Inc.

23. V.V. Sveics, *Small Nation Survival* (New York: Exposition Press, 1969), p. 25.

24. See M. Singer, *Weak States in a World of Powers* (New York: Free Press, 1972), pp. 89-378.

25. D. Vital, *The Inequality of States*, p. 1.

26. Ibid.

27. A.B. Fox, *The Power of Small States: Diplomacy in World War II* (Chicago: University of Chicago Press, 1959), p. 187.

28. R.L. Rothstein, *Alliances and Small Powers* (New York: Columbia University Press, 1968), pp. 34-6.

29. Richard W. Van Wagenen, *Research in the International Organization Field: Some Notes on Possible Focus* (Princeton, Center for Research on World Political Institutions, 1952), pp. 10-11.

30. K.W. Deutsch, 'Security Communities,' *International Politics and Foreign Policy*, ed. J.N. Rosenan (New York: The Free Press of Glencoe, 1961), pp. 99-100.

5   THE STRATEGIC IMPORTANCE OF THE GULF: US AND SOVIET FOREIGN POLICY

Because of its energy resources and location, and for economic, cultural, and religious reasons, the Gulf has become increasingly important to the Western world and to the Soviet Union in recent years. As David D. Newsom, then US Under-Secretary of State for Political Affairs, put it in a 1980 speech:

> If the world were a flat circle and one were looking for its center, a good argument could be made that it would lie in the Gulf. . . Nowhere in the world today is there quite such a convergence of global interests. No area is quite as central to the continued economic health and stability of the world.[1]

The Energy Dimension

The Gulf states are the main suppliers of oil to Western Europe (two-thirds of Western Europe's oil comes from the Gulf), Japan, and to a lesser extent the United States.[2] In 1981, the Gulf states

Table 5.1: Major Gulf Countries' Oil Output as Percentage of Regional and World Production, 1981

	Percentage of Gulf Output (rounded)	Percentage of World Output
Saudi Arabia	63.3	17.0
Iran	8.3	2.3
Iraq	5.7	1.5
Kuwait	6.1	1.7
Abu Dhabi	7.2	1.9
Qatar	2.6	0.7
Neutral Zone	1.9	0.7
Oman	2.0	0.5
Dubai	2.3	0.6
Total World Production		26.9

Source: *BP Statistical Review of the World Oil Industry* (1981).

56

accounted for 30.1 percent of total world oil production (see Table 5.1).

As the following table of 1981 world-wide proved oil reserves indicates, the Gulf region's share of the world total was about 53.5 percent. (Also significant is the Gulf's share [26.2 percent] of the world's natural gas reserves.)

The securing of Gulf oil is of utmost importance to many world leaders and their allies; the dependence of Western Europe and Japan upon Gulf oil, for example, is of great concern to the United States as well. It is anticipated that Gulf oil will also be of vital interest to the Soviet Union if, as some studies project, Soviet oil supplies begin to run short by the end of the 1980s.[3]

The Cultural and Religious Dimension

The Arabian Peninsula is the heart of Islam, the place where Arab and Islamic culture has flourished and to which Arabs trace their origin. The cities of Mecca and Medina in Saudi Arabia are the spiritual centers for more than 800 million people throughout the world. Each year, close to 2 million of them travel to Mecca to perform the *hajj*, one of the basic requirements of the Islamic faith. Kerbela and Najaf, in Iraq, represent the second most holy places for the Shi'ite sect of Islam. The holy sites, the most important of which are under the guardianship of Saudi Arabia, contribute substantially to the area's importance.

Table 5.2: World Proved Oil Reserves, 1980

Countries and Areas	Billion Barrels (bb)	% of Total
Gulf countries	362.0	53.5
North America	39.2	6.6
Latin America	69.5	12.5
Western Europe	23.2	3.7
Africa	55.1	8.3
USSR	63.0	9.3
Eastern Europe	2.8	0.4
China	20.5	2.9
Other Eastern Hemisphere	19.6	2.8

Source: *BP Statistical Review of the World Oil Industry* (1981).

Table 5.3: Gulf Oil Revenues, 1970-78 (In millions of US$)

	1970	1971	1972	1973	1974	1975	1976	1977	1978
Iran	1,136	1,944	2,380	4,100	17,500	18,500	22,000	21,300	20,500
Iraq	521	840	575	1,840	5,700	7,500	8,500	9,600	9,800
Kuwait	895	1,400	1,657	1,900	7,000	7,500	8,500	8,900	9,200
Qatar	122	198	255	410	1,600	1,700	2,000	2,000	2,000
Saudi Arabia	1,200	2,149	3,107	4,340	22,600	25,700	33,500	42,400	35,800
UAE	233	431	551	900	5,500	6,000	7,000	9,000	8,000

The Economic and Financial Dimension

Adding to the importance of the Gulf is the wealth of its major oil-producing states, which expanded in the wake of the increase in oil prices following the 1973 Arab-Israeli war and the oil embargo of the same year. Table 5.3 reveals the leap in oil-generated revenues from 1970 to 1978.

The bulk of the surplus capital from these revenues has been invested in dollar assets in banks in the United States as well as in their overseas branches and subsidiaries; such investment holdings were estimated to be between $150 and 250 billion for Saudi Arabia, Kuwait, the United Arab Emirates, and Qatar in 1981. Any attempt to withdraw a large portion of these assets from the United States would negatively affect the American economy and the international financial market and would provoke US defensive action. A Treasury Department official stated in 1979 that '. . . anticipated withdrawals of foreign assets of such magnitude as to threaten the economy and security of the US would justify the President's use of emergency powers . . . to block transfers of property in which there is foreign interests.'[4] In fact, the freezing of Iranian financial assets by the Carter administration on November 14, 1980 was not an act of retaliation against Iran because of that country's takeover of the US Embassy; instead it was undertaken out of fear that a sudden withdrawal of Iranian assets might contribute to a major economic crisis in the United States.[5]

The Geopolitical Dimension

The Gulf was important as a military and trade route as early as the time of the Mesopotamian civilization. In the third century BC, Alexander the Great realized the significance of the Gulf as a link between the western and eastern parts of his empire. He planned to conquer Arabia, regarding it as 'a vast tract inconveniently interposed between his Western and Eastern provinces.'[6] Nearchus, one of Alexander's trusted officers, was sent to explore the Gulf and a stone bearing a Greek inscription has been found on the north coast of Kuwait's Failaka Island. The inscription, Lockhart tells us:

. . . is believed to have been cut to commemorate the rescue from shipwreck of Soteles and his companion Oistra (who may have been his wife or slave). The date cannot be determined with exactitude, but it is thought to be between 400 and 100 BC. It is possible that the ship in which Soteles and Oistra were travelling when it was wrecked may have belonged to Nearchus' fleet, which reached the head of the Persian Gulf at the beginning of 325 BC.[7]

If this account is accurate, then we can safely assume that Alexander the Great was one of the first to see the Gulf as a bridge linking the continents.

The British presence in the Gulf, which began in the nineteenth century and lasted more than 100 years, underscores the region's geopolitical weight. It was not solely because of India that Britain held on so long; years after Britain relinquished its rule over the subcontinent, control over the Gulf was still maintained. The 1968 announcement of Britain's intention to withdraw from the Gulf by 1971 threw wide open one fo the world's richest and most strategic regions and created a dangerous power vacuum.[8] Today, the superpowers are engaged in rivalry over the region — a contest which, as far as the United States is concerned, became serious during the Carter administration following the Russian invasion of Afghanistan in 1979 and which intensified further after the election of Ronald Reagan as president in 1980.

The Superpowers and the Gulf: US Policy

From the 'containment' policy of the 1950s to the 'strategic consensus'[9] of the Reagan administration, US foreign policy in the Gulf, based on using surrogates to counter Soviet threats to US interests, has precipitated an arms race among the states in the region that threatens their very existence.

At the time of the British withdrawal from the Gulf in 1971, the United States used Iran as a proxy and sold it billions of dollars worth of arms to defend US interests in the Gulf. The Shah, seizing the opportunity presented to him by the British withdrawal and the offer of American help, sought to fulfill his dream of becoming the guardian of the Gulf. In world-wide press interviews, coupled with shows of force, including intervention in Oman, the

Shah tried to impress powers in and outside the Gulf with his strength and his intention of assuming a policeman's role on behalf of the US government. His insatiable appetite for more modern weapons and the US readiness to satisfy it were major factors contributing to the destruction of his regime by Khomeini. Ramazani, commenting on the Shah's demise, notes: '. . . there is little doubt that these unrestrained arms transactions contributed to [the Iranian revolution's] outbreak by diverting badly needed funds from social and economic projects and by placing unprecedented burdens on Iranian skilled manpower resources and economic and communication infrastructures.'[10]

US support of the Shah's armament build-up triggered an arms race all over the Gulf and the Arabian Peninsula. Table 5.4 shows the recent military expenditures of seven Gulf states. With US arms sales to the Gulf increasing 3,600 percent from 1970 to 1975, the United States could be said to be a major beneficiary of the Gulf region's arms race. US arms sales to the region, which in 1970 totaled $128 million, had reached $4.5 billion by 1975. These sales, which constituted 46 percent of total world-wide arms sales in 1975,[11] reached more than $5 billion in fiscal year 1980.[12]

It is thus apparent that the United States has benefitted in direct proportion to the increased insecurity of the region. Some would even argue that the US military complex is deliberately stoking turmoil in this very sensitive part of the world to encourage the

Table 5.4: Military Expenditures of Gulf States as Percentage of GNP, 1979 (Million Constant 1978 US$)

Country	Military Expenditures	GNP[a]	Percentage
Bahrain	53	1,874	2.8
Iran	NA	65,336	NA
Iraq	2,550	31,959	8.0
Kuwait	906	24,168	3.7
Oman	510	2,208	23.1
Qatar	1,161	3,164	36.7
Saudi Arabia	13,240	70,333	18.8

Note: a. In million dollars.
Source: US Arms Control and Disarmament Agency, *World Military Expenditures and Arms Transfers, 1970-1979.*

recycling of petrodollars through arms purchases. Whether this last notion is suspicion or fact, the almost limitless transfer of arms to the Gulf may itself be a destabilizing factor.[13] In any case, there can be no question that it is in the interest of the US military complex to encourage fears within these states, especially with regard to the Soviet Union. An objective of US foreign policy in the Gulf region is, therefore, to emphasize such dangers and simultaneously to secure larger arms purchases. Official US policy statements on the Gulf, however, downplay the role of arms transfers and declare US policy in the Gulf to be:

> support for collective security and stability in the region by encouraging indigenous regional cooperation efforts and orderly economic progress, continued access to the region's oil supplies . . . [and] enhancing of our commercial and financial interests.[14]

Popular suspicion of the United States in the region is sufficiently deep that any close relationship or identification on the part of the Gulf governments with American interests or security projects will in the long run only result in the alienation of populations from their own governments, with consequences that might well be similar to what happened in Iran. Nor is Iran the only case in point. One of the major factors contributing to the downfall of Iraq's General Nuri Said in 1958 was his support of the US-sponsored Baghdad Pact; he was killed only six months after his meeting with John Foster Dulles in Washington in December 1957. President Sadat of Egypt met his downfall after aligning himself with the US-sponsored Camp David Accords. His death was attributed to a group of Moslem fundamentalists, who alleged that Sadat's alliance with the United States and his signing of a peace treaty with Israel constituted an act of treason, not only to Egypt, but to the Islamic faith as well.

Recent events have put additional stresses on US-Gulf relations at the governmental as well as the grass roots level. The Israeli invasion of Lebanon on June 4, 1982, specifically in its initial stage, was seen by most Arabs as an act carried out with the full blessing of the US government. Repeated pleas from King Fahd to President Reagan conveyed the agonized feeling of Arabs in general and the Gulf states in particular with respect to American responsibility. The Saudi radio, according to the *New York Times* of August 6, 1982, stated that Reagan 'must do something more than petting Israel or bartering at the expense of two peoples who are being slaughtered.' It affirmed that King Fahd had asked President Reagan to 'shoulder his responsibility in full, for Arab patience has run out, and the Arabs are incapable of tolerating any more.' The impact of Israeli aggression in Lebanon may be devastating for the already shaky Arab-American relationship; during the summer of 1982 there was talk of a withdrawal of Arab assets from the United States or a new oil embargo. The threat of asset withdrawal was reiterated by Kuwait and Saudi Arabia, and the *New York Times* (August 6, 1982) quoted Arab diplomats to the effect that in July Saudi Arabia had threatened to withdraw over $100 billion deposited in US banks. Several members of the Kuwaiti parliament were reportedly trying to persuade the government to sever diplomatic and economic ties with the United States, suspend all oil shipments, and withdraw the country's billions of dollars of deposits presently in US banks.

US foreign policy in the Gulf is predicated upon the assumption that the USSR is the major threat to the area — especially to Western interests there. Such a policy is harmful because it downplays the real threat to the area emanating from the deadlock in the Arab-Israeli conflict, itself exacerbated by Israel's role as a US proxy and the US-sponsored Camp David Accords. Consequently, the policy will do nothing but increase tensions in the region. As long as the United States remains at the service of Israeli policy and seeks to apply a security model based on a surrogate presence, its role in the Gulf and in the Middle East is likely to remain constrained.

The Superpowers and the Gulf: Soviet Policy

In explaining the Soviet Union's role in the Gulf region, many writers point to the traditional Russian imperial design for a warm water port in the Gulf. Marlow states that:

> By the beginning of the 19th Century, Russia was already turning her eyes to the possibilities of colonizing Central Asia and of securing a warm water port in the Persian Gulf. The State of Persia at that time presented an obvious temptation to the furtherance of these two ambitions, both of which were viewed with great apprehension by the British as embodying the

unwelcome prospect of Russian expansion, both by land and by sea, in the direction of India. It may be said without serious exaggeration, that from the beginning of the 19th century, British policy in Persia and the Persian Gulf was conditioned principally by the existence of this apprehension.[15]

After Soviet intervention in Afghanistan in 1979, there was some concern that the search for new oil resources had been added to Russian designs for obtaining a warm water port.

Official Soviet policy toward the Gulf was discussed by the late President Leonid Brezhnev during his December 1980 visit to India. He suggested that the Soviet Union and the West jointly agree to the following proposals for peace and security in the Gulf: (1) No establishment of foreign military bases in the Persian Gulf or adjacent islands; no deployment of nuclear weapons in the region; (2) No use or threat of force against countries of the region or interference in their internal affairs; (3) Respect for the non-aligned status of Persian Gulf countries; no formation of military alliances in the region; (4) Respect for the right of sovereignty of Gulf countries over their natural resources; (5) No interference with trade in the Persian Gulf or with the use of maritime and other routes linking countries of the area with other parts of the world. In February 1981, during the 26th Congress of the Communist Party of the Soviet Union, the Soviets officially incorporated these proposals into a broad-based policy for the entire area and called for an international conference to settle outstanding issues between Moscow and Washington.

Generally speaking, Soviet influence has declined throughout the Middle East since the 1967 Arab-Israeli war and now the USSR's only real influence in the Gulf region is in the People's Democratic Republic of Yemen. What influence the Soviets used to have in Iraq has eroded as a result of the Iraqi-Iranian war; Iraq now looks more toward the West for fulfillment of its development programs.

The Soviet Union could, no doubt, strangle the West economically by taking control of the oil resources of the Gulf or by blocking the Straits of Hormuz through which most of Western Europe's and almost all of Japan's oil supplies pass. But the Soviet leaders also know that the economies of these states are of vital interest to the United States, and that any Soviet attempt to intervene in the Gulf region for the purpose of controlling oil production or exports would risk a serious confrontation between the two superpowers.

The Need for Stability

The Gulf region is wracked by tensions of its own which are only exacerbated by superpower meddling.[16] Simmering disputes have included the ideological confrontations between the radical regime of Iraq and the conservative regime of Kuwait, and between the conservative regime of Saudi Arabia and the radical government of the People's Democratic Republic of Yemen, as well as a number of smaller unresolved border controversies. The most serious present conflict within the region, however, is the war between Iraq and Iran which broke out in September 1980. This struggle has added to the existing strains among Arab states. While Jordan, Egypt, and the Arab states of the Gulf have supported Iraq, the Rejectionist Front, comprising Syria, Libya, Algeria, South Yemen, and the PLO, has opposed Iraq in the war and has declared that Iran is a friend of the Arabs. In the face of continuing Iranian threats, the Arab Gulf states have poured an estimated $22 billion into Iraq's war effort.

The Gulf states urgently need to develop comprehensive social, health, and welfare programs for their peoples and can ill afford the price of US and Soviet armaments, the dependence on foreign trainers and advisers these arms create, or the tensions and outright warfare that have followed their introduction into the region. The people of the Gulf feel that the pro-Western policies of their governments are not in their best interests. If an acceptable solution to the Palestinian problem fails to materialize, Gulf governments might lose legitimacy in the eyes of the governed, and this in turn might lead to popular uprisings. An uprising fueled by anti-Western sentiment in any of the Gulf states would, no doubt, represent a golden opportunity for Soviet intervention, especially if, as was the case with Afghanistan in 1979, such intervention were invited. Stability in the Gulf can only be attained through the achievement of a just and durable peace for the Palestinian people and through an integrated regional economic and defense plan, the major goal of the newly established Gulf Cooperation Council discussed in the next chapter.

Notes

1. D.D. Newsom, 'United States Policy Toward the Gulf,' *The United States, Arabia, and the Gulf*, ed. R.G. Wolfe (Washington, DC: Center for Contemporary Arab Studies (Georgetown University), 1980), p. 59. Mr Newsom is the former US Under Secretary of State for Political Affairs.

2. In 1979, the US imported 28.4 percent of its crude and product requirements from the Gulf countries, another 0.8 percent from Egypt and Syria, and 17 percent from Libya and Algeria.

3. A study submitted to the US Congress in July 1981 by the Defense Intelligence Agency contradicts the 1979 CIA report stating that the USSR will face an oil shortage in the 1990s. The DIA study shows a highly favorable outlook for oil in the Soviet Union due to the production in the huge al Salym oil field in Siberia. Soviet oil production is expected to rise to above 12 mbd in the 1980s and rise again in the 1990s. *Washington Post*, September 3, 1981.

4. A.I. Bloomfield and R.C. Marson, 'Policies for an OPEC Dollar Run,' *Journal of Post Keynesian Economics*, Vol. III, No. 3 (Spring 1981), pp. 300-2.

5. For details, see K. Lissakers, 'Money Manipulation,' *Foreign Policy*, No. 44 (Fall 1981), pp. 107-26.

6. G. Rawlinson, *Ancient History from the Earliest Times to the Fall of the Western Empire* (New York: Colonial Press, 1900), p. 175.

7. L. Lockhart, 'Outline of the History of Kuwait,' *Journal of the Royal Central Asian Society*, 34 (July–Oct. 1947), p. 262.

8. Following the British announcement of withdrawal, the Center for Strategic and International Studies of Georgetown University in Washington, DC, in a report concerning the Gulf and the implications of British withdrawal, listed three dangers confronting the Gulf: disturbance within the states themselves, conflict between the states, and the growth of influence of other powers in the Gulf (*The Gulf: Implications of British Withdrawal*, Georgetown University, 1969, pp. 7-8). For more details concerning disputes between the various Gulf states see W.D. Swearingen, 'Sources of Conflict Over Oil in the Persian/Arabian Gulf,' *The Middle East Journal*, Vol. 35, No. 3 (Summer 1981), 315-30, and H.M. Albharna, *The Arabian Gulf States* (Beirut: Librairie du Liban, 1975).

9. The so-called 'strategic consensus' of the Reagan administration is based upon Henry Kissinger's philosophy of American global policies. Kissinger states that 'The United States is no longer in a position to operate programs globally; it has to encourage them. It can no longer impose its preferred solution; it must seek to evoke it. . . Our role will have to be to contribute to a structure that will foster the initiative of others. . . We can continue to contribute to defense and positive programs, but we must seek to encourage and not stifle a sense of local responsibility.' From H.A. Kissinger, *American Foreign Policy*, Expanded edn (New York: N.W. Norton and Company, Inc., 1974), p. 93.

10. R.K. Ramazani, 'Security in the Persian Gulf,' *Foreign Affairs*, 57 (Spring 1979), p. 824.

11. US House of Representatives, Committee on International Relations, *The Persian Gulf, 1975: The Continuing Debate on Arms Sales. Hearings, Special Subcommittee on Investigations*, 94th Congress, 1st Session, 1975 (Washington, DC: US Government Printing Office, 1976), pp. 19-26.

12. US Department of Defense Security Assistance Agency, *Foreign Military Sales and Military Assistance Facts* (Washington, DC: US Department of Defense Security Assistance Agency, 1980).

13. Ramazani, 'Security in the Persian Gulf,' p. 825.

14. Ibid., p. 3. See also US House of Representatives, *New Perspectives on the*

Persian Gulf. Committee on Foreign Affairs, *Hearings, Subcommittee on the Near East and South Asia*, 93rd Congress, 1st Session, 1973 (Washington, DC: US Government Printing Office, 1973), p. 2.

15. J. Marlowe, *The Persian Gulf in the Twentieth Century* (London: The Crescent Press, 1962), pp. 18-19.

16. 'Two nationalisms and two kinds of political systems confront each other head on in the Persian Gulf.' D.E. Long, *Confrontation and Cooperation in the Gulf*, Middle East Problem Paper (Washington, DC: Middle East Institute, 1974).

6 THE GULF COOPERATION COUNCIL

Historical Background

Although the Kuwaiti government maintained at the time that there would be no power vacuum after the British withdrew from the Gulf,[1] the fact remains that Kuwait knew such a vacuum would occur and was very concerned that it would affect her security. While Kuwait had always been a supportive neighbor with a long history of aid to the smaller sheikhdoms, it was partly due to her fear of the consequences of British withdrawal that Kuwait began an intensive effort to facilitate and promote federation and integration in the area.

One way in which Kuwait's interest in regional bridge-building manifests itself is her past and present support for the United Arab Emirates. The first federation in modern Arab history, the UAE received invaluable assistance from Kuwait in the early days of its formation. Kuwaiti endorsement of the proposed federation — initially to be composed of Bahrain, Qatar, Abu Dhabi, Sharjah, Ajman, Umm Al-Qaiwain, Ras Al-Khaimah, Dubai, and Fujairah — prompted the rulers of these entities to engage in consultations with Kuwaiti leaders that eventually led to the signing of a federation agreement in 1971 (without the participation of Bahrain and Qatar).

While Saudi Arabia favored the federation, Iraq and the United Arab Republic gave only reluctant approval. Syria was the only Arab state to denounce the federation in strong terms; it subsequently reversed this position. The United States, together with Britain, expressed strong support, but the Soviet Union, while not opposing the creation of the UAE *per se*, 'criticized the venture as a manifestation of a residual British imperial presence.'[2]

As international tensions and superpower rivalry in the region increased after the British withdrawal, Kuwait again took the lead in establishing closer ties among the Gulf states. The establishment of a Gulf University was proposed in early 1980 during a visit by the Kuwaiti prime minister to the other Gulf states. Later in the year, an agreement on founding the university was signed in Kuwait by seven Gulf states — Saudi Arabia, Iraq, Kuwait,

Oman, UAE, Qatar, and Bahrain.

In early 1981, Kuwait's foreign minister submitted to the Gulf governments a working paper proposing the establishment of a Gulf Cooperation Council, and on February 4 of the same year the foreign ministers of the UAE, Bahrain, Oman, Saudi Arabia, Qatar, and Kuwait met in Riyadh, Saudi Arabia, to draw up an organizational structure for the proposed council. Out of this meeting came the Council Charter from which the following is taken:

> In recognition of the special ties which bind each of the UAE, Bahrain, Saudi Arabia, Oman, Qatar and Kuwait to one another, arising from their common ideology and heritage and the similarity between their social, political and demographic structure, and out of desire to promote their people's prosperity, growth and stability through closer cooperation, the foreign ministers of these states met in Riyadh, Saudi Arabia on February 4, 1981. The talks at this meeting were aimed at drawing up a practical framework for the consolidation and development of cooperation between the states concerned. As a result it was decided to establish a Cooperation Council between these Arab Gulf States which would have a general secretariat and hold regular meetings, both on the summit and foreign minister level in order to achieve the goals of the states and their peoples in the fields.[3]

Those who wrote the Charter included language aimed at allaying potential Arab opposition:

> This step conforms with the national aims of the Arab Nation as expressed in the Charter of the Arab League, which encourages regional cooperation as a means of strengthening the Nation. In this way, the formation of the Gulf Cooperation Council can be seen as confirming the support of these states for the Arab League, its Charter and objective, and Islam as a whole.

On the same day, a description of the Council structure and purpose (see Appendix A at the end of this chapter for details) was released:

> In recognition of the special ties, common characteristics and

similar institutions linking each of the UAE, Bahrain, Saudi Arabia, Oman, Qatar and Kuwait, and due to the importance of establishing close cooperation in all fields, particularly economic and social, the aforementioned states see a need for the establishment of an organization aimed at strengthening the ties and cooperation between them in all its spheres. This organization, to be known as the Gulf Cooperation Council, shall have its headquarters in Riyadh, Saudi Arabia. It shall be a means of achieving a greater degree of coordination and integration in all fields and of forging closer relations between its members. To this end it will form corresponding organizations in the fields of economics and finance, education and culture, social affairs and health, communications, information and media, nationality and passports, travel and transportation, commerce, customs and the movement of goods, and finally in legal and administrative affairs.

At the conclusion of this initial meeting, the foreign ministers of the six states agreed to hold their next summit meeting in Muscat, Oman, beginning on March 8, 1981. This was preceded by two organizational meetings on February 24 and March 4, 1981, in Riyadh and Muscat respectively, at which a proposed structure for the Gulf Cooperation Council was formulated. The draft was ratified by the Muscat summit meeting on March 10, thereby making the Gulf Cooperation Council a reality. Abdulla Bishara, former Kuwaiti ambassador to the United Nations, was elected to be the Council's first Secretary-General.

Demographic Constraints

The Council, the major goal of which is the ultimate federation of all the Gulf states, consists of six countries whose total population is about 13 million and whose total GNP is estimated at $113.55 billion. However, each of the member states faces serious weaknesses and constraints implicit in the presence of vast numbers of alien elements amid a small indigenous population. The following demographic survey of the six countries indicates the extent of the problem.

Kuwait

The 1976 census placed the population of Kuwait at 1,093,900, of which 52.7 percent were non-Kuwaitis. In one year the population had increased by nearly 10 percent over the 1975 total of 994,837. The population density in 1976 was 64.5 people per square kilometer. Two aspects of the population distribution are especially noteworthy. First, in many areas citizens and immigrants live apart. The governorate of Hawalli, for example, is primarily inhabited by Palestinians. Second, Kuwaitis generally live in suburbia, while non-Kuwaitis live in the crowded and less well-planned inner cities.

Prior to the first census of 1957, there was no precise knowledge of the population of Kuwait but it was estimated at 50,000. The 1957 population was assessed at about 206,473, but by 1965 it had reached 467,339; this means that the average annual increase in population over the intervening period amounted to almost 16 percent of the initial population. The corresponding figures for 1965-70 and 1970-7 are 12 percent and 6.9 percent. Kuwait's growth rate is thus one of the highest in the world — making planning extremely difficult — and the population may well double within a decade.

A major factor in Kuwait's rapid growth is immigration. The early immigrants of the late 1940s and early 1950s were mostly Iraqis, Iranians, Omanis, and Palestinians. In 1957, Iraqis constituted 28 percent of Kuwait's population, Iranians 21 percent, and Palestinians 16 percent. By 1975, however, Palestinians constituted about two-fifths of the non-Kuwaiti population. While this shift was accompanied by a drastic drop in the number of Iraqis living in Kuwait, Egyptians and Syrians have steadily increased in numbers. (The percentage of non-Kuwaitis in the total population rose in the 1980 census to about 58 percent.) Tables 6.1, 6.2, 6.3 and 6.4 provide further information about the population of Kuwait.

Saudi Arabia

There are no exact figures on Saudi Arabia's population. The 1974 census put the population at 7,012,642 and the government estimate in 1980 was 8,224,000, but these figures may be too high; according to some unofficial estimates, the population is about 5.5 million; this includes about 1.5 million non-Saudis, 1 million of whom are Yemenis. According to the 1974 census, the population

Table 6.1: Kuwaiti Population by Governorates by Sex and Nationality (1980 Census)[b]

Governorate	Total population			Non-Kuwaitis			Kuwaitis[a]		
	Total	Female	Male	Total	Female	Male	Total	Female	Male
Capital	131,774	68,782	112,992	110,321	32,360	77,961	71,453	36,422	35,031
Hawalli	750,713	319,453	431,260	545,853	216,463	379,390	204,360	102,990	101,870
Ahmade	232,167	103,617	128,550	96,537	34,727	61,810	135,630	68,890	66,740
Jahra	189,971	87,829	102,142	39,849	12,582	27,267	150,122	75,247	74,875
Transits	1,202	21	1,181	1,202	21	1,181	–	–	–
Grand Total	1,355,827	579,702	776,125	793,762	296,153	497,609	562,065	283,549	278,516

Notes: a. Excluded Kuwaitis residing abroad; b. Preliminary results; c. New Governorate.

Source: Kuwait Ministry of Planning, Central Statistical Office, *Annual Statistical Abstract*, 1981.

Table 6.2: Foreign Nationals in Kuwait, 1975

Nationality	Number	Percentage of Total Population	Percentage of Foreign Population
All Arabs	419,187	42.1	80.2
Jordanian/ Palestinian	204,178	20.5	39.0
Egyptian	60,534	6.1	11.6
Iraqi	45,070	4.5	8.6
Syrian	40,962	4.1	8.0
Other Arabs	67,843	6.9	13.0
Non-Arabs	103,562	10.4	19.8
Iranian	40,842	4.1	8.0
Indian	32,105	3.2	6.1
Pakistani	23,016	2.3	4.4
All others	2,599	0.8	1.3
Total	522,749	52.2	100.0

Source: Kuwait Ministry of Planning, Central Statistical Office, *Annual Statistical Abstract*, 1976.

Table 6.3: Population of Kuwait by Age Group, Sex, and Nationality, 1975

Age Group	Sex	Kuwaitis	Non-Kuwaitis	Total
0-14	M	118,017	106,043	224,114
	F	115,371	101,422	216,793
Total (%)		233,442 (23.4%)	207,465 (20.9%)	440,907 (44.3%)
15-29	M	59,577	83,209	142,786
	F	65,108	57,844	122,952
Total (%)		124,685 (12.6%)	141,053 (14.1%)	265,738 (26.7%)
30-49	M	40,461	101,356	141,817
	F	37,394	47,001	84,395
Total (%)		77,855 (7.7%)	148,357 (15.0%)	226,212 (22.7%)
50+	M	18,491	16,560	35,051
	F	17,615	9,314	26,929
Total (%)		36,106 (3.7%)	25,874 (2.6%)	61,980 (6.3%)
Total	M	236,600	306,168	534,768
	F	235,488	215,581	451,069
Grand Total[a] (%)		472,088 (47.5%)	522,749 (52.5%)	994,837 (100%)

Note: a. Percentages do not agree with Grand Total due to rounding off.
Source: Kuwait Ministry of Planning, Central Statistical Office, *Annual Statistical Abstract*, 1976.

Table 6.4: Numbers Employed in Economic Sectors in Kuwait, 1975

Sectors	Kuwaitis	Non-Kuwaitis
Agriculture	3,983	3,531
Mining	1,779	3,083
Industry	2,258	22,209
Construction	1,576	30,500
Utilities	2,034	5,234
Trade	6,327	33,232
Transport/Communication	4,567	11,118
Services	64,265	102,537
Other	1	–
Total	86,971	211,444

Source: Kuwait Ministry of Planning, Central Statistical Office, *Annual Statistical Abstract,* 1976.

density was 3.2 people per square kilometer, with the settled population put at 5,128,655 (73.1 percent) and nomads at 1,883,987 (26.9 percent). Increased urban migration has contributed to the steady growth of Riyadh, Jidda, Mecca, Dammam, and Tabuk (see Table 6.5).

Table 6.5: Population of the Major Cities of Saudi Arabia

City	Population
Riyadh	666,840
Jidda	561,104
Mecca	366,801
Taif	204,857
Medina	198,186
Dammam	127,844
Hufuf	101,271

Source: Kingdom of Saudi Arabia, Central Department of Statistics, *The Statistical Indicator,* 1976.

There are no detailed statistics available concerning the numbers of people in different age groups. UN estimates put the annual growth rate at about 3 percent during 1970-5.

Bahrain

The population of Bahrain was about 373,000 in 1980. According to the census of 1971, the population was 216,078, 82.5 percent of which was Bahraini and 17.5 percent non-Bahraini. About 78.1 percent of the population was urban, with the majority inhabiting Manama, the capital; 21.9 percent was rural. The annual growth rate during 1941-50 was 2.6 percent. The annual growth increased to 3 percent during 1950-8 and to 3.3 percent during 1959-71. The 1971-5 growth rate was 5.6 percent. Tables 6.6, 6.7 and 6.8 present further data on Bahrain's population.

Table 6.6: Population of Bahrain by Urban-rural Location and Nationality, 1971

	Bahrainis	Non-Bahrainis	Total
Manama Division	59,496	29,903	89,399
Manama Town	58,884	29,901	88,785
Rural	612	2	614
Muharraq Island	45,774	3,766	49,540
Muharraq Town	34,112	3,620	37,732
Hidd Town	5,172	97	5,269
Rural	6,490	49	6,539
Jiddhafs Division	19,065	456	19,521
Jiddhafs Town	10,743	409	11,152
Rural	8,322	47	8,369
Northern Division (rural)	10,454	160	10,614
Western Division (rural)	8,355	334	8,869
Central Division	13,946	286	14,228
Isa Town	7,285	216	7,501
Rural	6,661	66	6,727
Sitra Division	11,263	60	11,323
Sitra Town	6,624	41	6,665
Rural	4,639	19	4,658
Riffa Division	9,766	2,867	12,633
Riffa Town	9,171	1,560	10,731
Awali Town	24	960	984
Rural	571	347	918
Other Islands	74	57	131
Total	178,193	37,885	216,078
Urban	132,015	36,804	168,819
Rural	46,178	1,081	47,259

Source: State of Bahrain, Ministry of Finance and National Economy, Statistical Bureau, *Statistics of the Population Census*, 1971.

Table 6.7: Population of Bahrain by Age Group, Sex, and Nationality, 1971

Age Group	Sex	Bahrainis	Non-Bahrainis	Total
0-14	M	43,258	4,894	48,152
	F	43,088	4,400	47,488
Total (%)		86,346 (39.9%)	9,294 (4.3%)	95,640 (44.2%)
15-29	M	21,244	9,047	30,291
	F	21,039	3,250	24,289
Total (%)		42,283 (19.6%)	12,297 (5.6%)	54,580 (25.2%)
30-44	M	12,109	8,948	21,057
	F	12,760	2,597	15,357
Total (%)		24,869 (11.5%)	11,545 (5.4%)	36,414 (16.9%)
45-59	M	8,584	2,889	11,473
	F	7,151	795	7,946
Total (%)		15,735 (7.2%)	5,684 (1.8%)	19,419 (9%)
60+	M	4,577	764	5,341
	F	4,383	301	4,684
Total (%)		8,960 (4.1%)	1,065 (0.5%)	10,025 (4.6%)
Grand Total	M	89,772	26,542	116,314
	F	88,421	11,343	99,764
Total[a] (%)		178,193 (82.5%)	37,885 (17.5%)	216,078 (100%)

Note: a. Percentages do not add up due to rounding off.
Source: State of Bahrain, Ministry of Finance and National Economy, Statistical Bureau, *Statistics of the Population Census*, 1971.

Table 6.8: Economically Active Population by Sector and Nationality, 1971

Sector	Bahrainis	Non-Bahrainis	Total
Agriculture, Fishing	2,995	995	3,990
Mining, Manufacturing	5,614	2,850	8,464
Utilities	1,480	225	1,705
Construction	5,639	4,765	10,404
Trade	4,851	2,855	7,706
Transportation, Communication	5,067	2,676	7,706
Finance, Business	740	344	1,804
Services	10,930	7,458	18,388
Other	634	183	817
Total	37,950	22,351	60,301

Source: State of Bahrain, Ministry of Finance and National Economy, Statistical Bureau, *Statistics of the Population Census*, 1971.

Qatar

The population of Qatar in 1980 was an estimated 250,000, with a density of about 20 per square kilometer. More than 180,000 live in the capital city, Doha. The remainder are largely located in Dukhan, Umm Said, and other small towns. The annual growth rate — 3 percent for the natives and 5 percent for foreigners — is largely due to immigration in conjunction with the oil-based economic boom. The number of native Qataris is estimated at no more than 80,000; in 1940, there were an estimated 12,000. Foreigners living in Qatar are chiefly from Pakistan, Iran, Egypt, and Lebanon and comprise over 80 percent of Qatar's work force.

United Arab Emirates

The population of the UAE was given in the 1980 census to be 1,040,275. The total obtained in the 1975 census was 655,937, with the figures for each emirate as follows: Abu Dhabi, 449,000; Dubai, 278,000; Sharjah, 159,000; Ras Al-Khaimah, 73,700; Ajman, 36,100; Umm Al-Qaiwain, 12,300; and Fujairah, 32,200. The population density is 13.4 per square kilometer. The great increase in population over the 1968 total of 180,184 is essentially due to the immigration of foreign laborers. The foreign populace now totals about 525,000, three-quarters of whom are Pakistanis, Indians, and Iranians. The remainder are mostly Arabs and Westerners. The total annual growth of the population is about 22 percent, of which a little over 2.5 percent represents increase in the indigenous population. The majority of people in Abu Dhabi and Dubai live in towns, while the northern emirates are less urbanized and have fewer foreign laborers.

Oman

Government estimates put the population of Oman at about 930,000, while unofficial estimates place it at 600,000. The population density is about 2 per square kilometer. More than 80,000 reside in Muscat (the capital) and in the cities of Matra and Sib; 50,000 live in Salala. Other concentrations can be found in the Batina coastal plain and in the interior, in such towns as Nizwa. There is no shortage of native manpower in Oman (which has about 60,000 Indian and Pakistani workers) comparable to that in Qatar and the UAE. About 75 percent of the work force is employed in agriculture.

Table 6.9: Defense Spending and Capabilities of Gulf Co-operation Council Members, 1981

Kuwait

Total armed forces	:	12,400
Paramilitary forces	:	18,000 police
Defense expenditure	:	$1.3 billion (1981)
Army	:	10,000
Navy	:	500
Air force	:	1,900

Saudi Arabia

Total armed forces	:	52,200
Paramilitary forces	:	31,500
Defense expenditure	:	$24.4 billion
Army	:	35,000
Navy	:	2,200
Air force	:	15,000

Oman

Total armed forces	:	18,000 (excluding expatriate personnel)
Paramilitary forces	:	3,300 Tribal Home Guard 1,200 Royal Guard Regiment
Defense expenditure	:	$1.69 billion
Army	:	15,000 regular
Navy	:	1,000
Air force	:	2,000

Bahrain

Total armed forces	:	2,550
Paramilitary forces	:	Police detachments: 2,680
Defense expenditure	:	$135 million
Army	:	2,300
Navy	:	150
Air force	:	100

Qatar

Total armed forces	:	6,000
Paramilitary forces	:	None
Defense expenditure	:	$893.1 million
Army	:	5,000
Navy	:	700 (including marine police)
Air force	:	300

United Arab Emirates

Total armed forces	:	48,500
Paramilitary forces	:	None
Defense expenditure	:	$1.2 billion (1980)
Army	:	46,000
Navy	:	1,000
Air force	:	1,500

Defense Capabilities

The small size of the Gulf's population and the region's extreme dependence upon oil makes the area a vulnerable one. Thus, the Gulf governments have given defense spending increased priority, as the figures in Table 6.9 show.[4]

While the Gulf states themselves would not be able to defend their territory beyond complicating or delaying the first wave of an external attack, it has been argued by US military authorities that such a capability as is being developed will make it more difficult 'for the Soviet airborne forces to sweep into the Gulf ahead of advancing ground units, seizing airfields, and other installations upon which US projection forces would depend for their own entry.'[5] It is thus clear that from the US point of view heavy expenditure on armaments on the part of the Gulf states is justified because of the possibility of a Soviet assault, even though few in the region consider such an attack likely.

Oil and Financial Assets

In 1980, the states now constituting the Gulf Cooperation Council produced an estimated 23.1 percent of total world oil output and about 77.6 percent of combined Gulf region oil production; they held oil reserves amounting to 53.5 percent of the world total.[6] As of June 1981, the accumulated foreign assets of Saudi Arabia were some $150 billion, while those of Kuwait were approximately $72 billion.[7] Tables 6.10 and 6.11 show the growth of foreign assets and investment income for the two leading members of the Council, Saudi Arabia and Kuwait.[8]

Table 6.10: Foreign Assets (In US$ billions)

	1972	1977	1978	1979	1980	Jan-June 81	Est. end 1981
Kuwait	2.4	21	27	49	65	72	76
Saudi Arabia	2.3	64	61	78	125	150	175
Total	4.7	85	88	127	190	222	251

Table 6.11: Investment Income (In US$ billions)

	1972	1977	1978	1979	1980	Jan-June 81	Est. end 1981
Kuwait	0.410	2.1	2.7	4.8	6.5	not available	7.6
Saudi Arabia	0.125	4.4	6.4	7.8	12.5	not available	17.5
Total	0.535	6.5	9.1	12.6	19.0		25.1

Chances for Success

Although the Gulf states have excellent economic potential, supported by good transport and communications networks, the achievement of the ultimate goal of the Gulf Cooperation Council — the social and economic integration of all the Gulf states — depends upon success in transcending the internal and external obstacles discussed below.

Internal Obstacles

Political Underdevelopment. The member states of the Gulf Cooperation Council (except for Kuwait) lag far behind in terms of their political institutional development. In most, no formula has been devised for participatory government. Bahrain has yet to return to parliamentarian government and the much-discussed Saudi constitution has yet to materialize. Many constitutional issues remain unresolved in the UAE and in some instances political differences have resulted in military clashes between various sheikhdoms. Oman faces the prospect of a renewed uprising in Dhofar province and the Bahraini-Qatari border dispute remains unsettled. Restrictions on the press, judicial systems, and individual freedom and economic opportunity differ greatly from one state to another. If popular discontent is to be avoided and integration is to become possible, a concerted effort must be undertaken to rectify the political imbalance and underdevelopment in the six states. Kuwait's experience with parliamentary government will undoubtedly be beneficial in the connection.[9]

Uneven Social Development. While women's rights are recognized or in the process of being recognized in some of the Council states, the women's rights movement is still in its infancy in most of them.

Likewise, there are well-developed urban centers in some states, while others contain large numbers of members of unsettled tribes. Almost all of the states rely heavily upon foreign workers and experts, and this exposes them to serious social tensions and uncertainty about the future.

Educational and Manpower Training Problems. The small Gulf states with vast, exhaustible natural resources face a bleak future unless their human resources are developed. The situation in these states is exacerbated by the necessity of relying to an increasing extent upon foreign labor. Expatriates work in many if not all government agencies throughout the Gulf; there is even a substantial amount of reliance upon mercenaries in the armed forces.

The major problem faced by the Gulf states in increasing their supplies of skilled native manpower lies in the area of education. In each Gulf Cooperation Council state, the educational system has been molded under the influence of the Egyptian system. The Saudis were the first to launch a university in 1962, Kuwait followed in 1966, Bahrain in 1978, the University of the Gulf was opened in 1982 and the planning set in process for the Qabus University in Oman. With the exception of the Bahrain University College, they were developed on the Egyptian model. Most started with an Egyptian rector and staff and adopted the rules and regulations of either the Egyptian universities or the Egyptian Ministry of Higher Education. Most of these universities were established as a symbolic gesture emphasizing the autonomy and prestige of one or another newly independent state. Each was hastily conceived with very little planning. In short, the decision to establish a university was perhaps less the result of an extensive study of appropriate prerequisites for a modern university system than a manifestation of the desire to assert the state's independent identity.

To make matters worse, Egyptian bureaucratic procedures and curricula, unrelated to local environments and needs, have been adopted by these states. A case in point is the 1972 curriculum at the School of Commerce of the University of Kuwait. Graduation then required completing courses in agricultural economics (cotton-growing!). Likewise, there were railroad transportation courses offered but none for sea transportation or for oil economics.

Generally speaking, this approach to education emphasizes

memorization at the expense of analytical thinking. Students are in school essentially for the purpose of securing a diploma in the hope of entering the degree-stratified government bureaucracy. The organizational structure of the university is archaic and is headed by a non-native, usually Egyptian, rector. Real power within the university is held by the secretary-general, usually a national and from outside the academic community, who enjoys the confidence of the minister of education. By university law, the minister of education is also the president of the university and has unlimited powers in presiding over the university council. He can thus bypass and undermine the authority of the rector. The state has complete control in selecting not only the rector and the secretary-general, but also the deans and occasionally even heads of departments. In terms of management and operation, universities in the Arab Gulf states lack autonomy, are operated by the states, and are subject, with few exceptions, to the rules and regulations governing the civil service structure. Given these problems facing higher education, there is reason for pessimism about the ability of this system to meet the skilled manpower requirements associated with the development and economic integration of the Council member states.

How can this situation be rectified? To begin with we must look at the Arab world as a whole if we are to think of reforming higher education. Because Egypt — with 35 percent of the total population of the Arab world — will continue to supply a significant amount of the manpower required by the Gulf states, the basis of its higher education system must be revised. The Gulf states themselves must establish a unified university system, based on a comprehensive planning and admissions policy linked to the skilled manpower needs of the various states. The so-called open-door admissions policy must be ended; hard choices lie ahead. Whether the member states will choose the easy way based on political expedience or face up to the reality of difficult decisions, time will tell. But time is running out in this part of the Arab world.

External Obstacles

Intra-Arab Politics. The Arab world's reaction to the Gulf Cooperation Council is not yet fully apparent. However, there is a lingering suspicion in Syria that the Council is an idea inspired by a US strategic plan for the Gulf. (This is the same reaction Syria had toward the establishment of the UAE.) The Communist Party of the Soviet Union opposed the Council, charging in *Pravda* that it would be more concerned with military affairs than with expanding cooperation and that there was a link between the Council and NATO allies.[10] The Soviet Union's disapproval and Libya's suspicion were manifested by the signing of a Libyan-Ethiopian-South Yemeni friendship and cooperation treaty on August 18, 1981 by Colonel Qaddafi. According to the *Washington Post*, this treaty was described by Washington sources as a Libyan-bankrolled pact to confront US–allied countries in the area.[11] Kuwait's foreign minister attempted to counteract the fear of possible Council connections with an outside power by including on the Council's agenda a proposed Gulf Security Project, the purpose of which is described below:

> Gulf security is sort of collective participation in preserving the security of the region so that it should not be the sole responsibility of one state. Collective security is seen as the best means of ensuring the stability of the region since it is not directed against anyone in particular, but against all those who seek to disrupt the region's security. The enormous wealth and relatively small size of the states in the region makes them the object of covetous ambitions on the part of more powerful nations. The states of the region are faced with the choice of accepting the situation as it exists or of uniting and reinforcing their efforts in order to confront the challenge they face.[12]

China declared its support of the Council by responding to *Pravda*'s criticism in its official paper, *The People*.[13] In February 1981, the Arab League's Secretary-General, Chedlie Klibi, expressed approval of the Council, as did Morocco and Tunisia shortly thereafter. There was also general acceptance and support from London and Washington. Iraq's response to the Council has been positive. Though it has not so far been invited to join, Iraq must eventually be brought into the Council if the organization is to have real strength.

For the Council to succeed, it must avoid taking sides in inter- and intra-Arab conflicts and must play the role of an honest, unbiased intermediary. It must also solidify its support for a just settlement of the Arab-Israeli crisis and expand its efforts to help the poorer Arab countries in their economic development schemes.

Otherwise, the widening gap between the have and have-not Arab states will lead to social and political unrest in the poorer Arab countries which would have an immediate adverse impact on the Gulf region.[14]

It is true that the Gulf Cooperation Council may limit the kind of aid formerly given by individual states to appease certain Arab governments in return for support. This restriction might, however, prove a blessing; future aid might be better planned and directed toward more appropriate and cost-effective development projects. In the past, such aid has often landed in the pockets of the ruling elites.

Superpower Rivalry. In view of the fact that the Gulf region is an area of intense superpower rivalry, the Gulf Cooperation Council, if it is to succeed, must lay to rest any Russian fear that it is in alliance with the West. It should aim at neutralizing the Gulf region and endeavor to keep the superpowers out of this very sensitive and explosive area. As indicated before, any close relationships with the United States or the NATO countries would certainly bring about not only Arab governmental opposition to the Council but the opposition of the people in the various Council member states themselves.

Notes

1. Kuwait's foreign minister at the time immediately preceding British withdrawal presented his government's position as follows: 'The British must go by 1971 and the gap created by their departure will be filled by countries of the area.' See H.A. Al-Ebraheem, *Kuwait: A Political Study* (Kuwait: Kuwait University Press, 1975), pp. 143-8.

2. Robert H. Hunter, *The Soviet Dilemma in the Middle East, Part II: Oil and the Persian Gulf* (London: The International Institute for Strategic Studies (IISS), 1969), pp. 13-14 (Adelphi Papers No. 60).

3. Kuwait News Agency (KUNA), *Digest*, The Gulf Cooperation Council, May 1981, pp. 8-9.

4. The International Institute for Strategic Studies, *The Military Balance, 1982-1983* (London: IISS, 1982).

5. US House of Representatives, Committee on Foreign Affairs, *US Security Interests in the Persian Gulf: Report of a Staff Study Mission to the Persian Gulf, Middle East and Horn of Africa*, Oct. 21-Nov. 13, 1980 (Washington, DC: 1981), p. 91.

6. *Oil and Gas Journal*, BP Statistical Review of the World Oil Industry, 1981.

7. O. Oburdene, 'The Investment Income of Saudi Arabia and Kuwait' (June 1981), unpublished manuscript.

8. *Ibid.*, p. 5.
9. KUNA, The Gulf Cooperation Council (news release), February 16, 1981, p. 67.
10. See KUNA, p. 76.
11. *Washington Post*, August 20, 1981, p. A-17.
12. KUNA, *Digest*, The Gulf Cooperation Council, May 1981.
13. See KUNA, p. 79.
14. For details, see J.S. Birks and C.A. Sinclair, *Arab Manpower: The Crisis of Development* (New York: St Martin's Press, 1980). See also the excellent article of M.H. Kerr, 'Rich and Poor in the New Arab Order,' *Journal of Arab Affairs* (Oct. 1981), Vol. 1, 1-24; and S. Ibrahim, 'Superpowers in the Arab World,' *Washington Quarterly*, Vol. 4, No. 3 (Summer 1981), pp. 81-94.

Appendix : Organizational Structure of the Gulf Cooperation Council[1]

The Cooperation Council shall be composed of:

1. The Supreme Council comprising the Conciliation Commission.
2. The Ministerial Council.
3. The General Secretariat.

The Supreme Council:
1. Shall be composed of the heads of state.
2. Shall have a presidency which rotates in alphabetical order.
3. Shall hold two ordinary sessions every year with the possibility of holding extraordinary sessions as necessary.
4. Every member shall have the right to call a ministerial meeting so long as the call is seconded by at least one other member.

The Supreme Council's jurisdiction:
The Supreme Council shall determine the Cooperation Council's higher policies and the basic lines along which it operates. It shall discuss the recommendations, rules, and regulations submitted by the Ministerial Council and General Secretariat for approval. In addition, it shall appoint the Conciliation Commission.

The Conciliation Commission:
Annexed to the Supreme Council, this Commission shall be responsible for resolving existing or potential disputes among member states and for interpreting the Cooperation Council's basic regulations.

The Ministerial Council:
1. Shall be composed of the foreign ministers or their representatives.
2. Shall draw up the organizational structure of the General Secretariat.
3. Shall prepare for meetings of the Supreme Council, a function that includes compiling projects, studies, recommendations, and agendas.
4. Shall meet six times a year — once every two months — and shall hold extraordinary meetings as and when requested by at least two member states.
5. Shall formulate policies, recommendations, and studies and suggest projects aimed at promoting cooperation among the member states in different spheres.
6. Shall encourage various forms of cooperation and coordination in the different activities of the private sector.
7. Shall ratify the regular reports as well as the internal regulations relating to administrative affairs proposed by the Secretary-General. In addition, it shall approve the budget and final accounts of the Cooperation Council's General Secretariat.
8. Shall encourage, develop, and coordinate the various fields, since these activities will be considered binding once they are sanctioned by the Ministerial Council. It shall also charge relevant ministers with the formulation of policies and studies that aid the realization of the Cooperation Council's objective.

The General Secretariat:
The Cooperation Council shall be headed by a Secretary-General to be appointed by the Supreme Council which shall also determine the conditions and term of his office. It is a prerequisite that the Secretary-General be a subject of one of the member states. He shall be directly responsible for the functions of the Assistant Secretaries, the General Secretariat, and the progress of work in its various sectors. The General Secretariat shall have its own information bureau.
Functions of the General Secretariat:
1. Preparation of studies especially related to cooperation and coordination.
2. Following up the implementation of resolutions and recom-

mendations proposed by the member states, and ratified by the Supreme Council and the Ministerial Council.

3. Preparation of progress reports on the Cooperation Council's achievements.

4. Preparation of reports and studies requested by the Ministerial Council.

5. Drafting of financial and administrative regulations that help the organization develop in accordance with the growth of the Cooperation Council and its increasing responsibilities.

The General Secretariat Budget:
The Cooperation Council's General Secretariat shall have a budget to which all member states shall contribute equally.

Note

1. Kuwait News Agency (KUNA), *Digest*, 'The Gulf Cooperation Council,' May 1981, pp. 9-12.

7   KUWAIT: A SMALL STATE MODEL

The State of Kuwait can be viewed as an example of a small state, not only in the context of the Gulf region, but in the larger international system. Despite its small size, Kuwait has played an active role in Gulf politics in particular, and in inter-Arab politics in general. As the initiator of the Gulf Cooperation Council, it is the model which other Gulf states, correctly or incorrectly, aspire to imitate.

Kuwait Political Development

One of the major challenges facing newly emerged small states is the achievement of mature political development through national integration. Failure to achieve this goal has been paid at a very high price in ethnic or religious conflict and factional strife. In this respect Kuwait, which since its founding has been ruled as an hereditary emirate, has been particularly fortunate. The regime's legitimacy has not only been based on election and consultation but every effort has been made over the years to strengthen and nourish these popular bonds.

The tradition of consultation between the ruler and his subjects, however, is not an alien phenomenon in the Arabian Peninsula. On the contrary, it is one of the major pillars of tribal society although the degree of consultation has differed considerably from tribe to tribe. In general it can be said that the desert bedouin is something of a democrat in nature and strives to maintain his freedom of unfettered expression of opinion. While taught from early childhood to respect the opinions of their elders, bedouin children are also encouraged to voice their opinions on matters affecting tribal life.

After achieving independence in 1961 the Kuwait ruling family set out to institutionalize traditional consultation through a popularly elected National Assembly. The Assembly, once constituted, proceeded to play an important role in the state's economic, political and social development. The Assembly's positive impact was particularly felt in championing human rights, especially freedom of the press and free speech. Although the National Assembly was extra-constitutionally suspended in 1976, in large part the result of a regional political crisis, it was reconstituted in 1981 as an instrument and forum for popular opinion. However, in the view of some observers, the new Assembly, unlike its predecessor, has failed to take a strong stand on human rights. Not only has it rejected female suffrage but it has barred naturalization for non-Muslims. The wasting of time on minor issues at the expense of matters of major economic and political importance has also been cited as characteristic of the new Assembly. The overwhelming electoral defeat in 1981 of the 'unofficial' opposition from the previous Assembly has undoubtedly taken its toll on the development of the Kuwaiti polity.

Historical Background

Knowledge about Kuwait's history before the eighteenth century is limited to scattered bits of information and what has been found at a few archaeological sites on the island of Failaka.[1] The country's recorded history began in the eighteenth century with the arrival of the Utubi, a clan of the Anza tribe of north-central Arabia, who founded the town of Kuwait. Unlike the case in the neighboring Gulf states, where rulers were the by-product of intertribal struggles, the first Amir of the town was elected by the tribal council. (One might argue that this early elective tradition helps account for the political tolerance shown by the ruling family in Kuwait's later history.) Within a period of 50 years, the Utubi town grew in wealth and population and achieved some degree of political autonomy. The first population estimate of Kuwait, given by J.H. Stocqueler in 1832, was around 4,000 inhabitants.[2] The population in 1905 was some 35,000 and in 1919 about 85,000; the 1947 population was estimated at close to 120,000. Kuwait's size was closely tied to the fortunes of the small town, and the number of inhabitants increased or decreased according to the ebb and flow of trade and events in the surrounding area.

Kuwait gained in importance as a trading center because of Basrah's decline due to the plague of 1773-4 and the 1776 Persian occupation. It was during this time that Britain made its first official contact with Kuwait, a contact which subsequently proved crucial to Kuwait's survival. The advantage which redounded to

Kuwait from the tragedy of Basrah is well summarized by Professor Abu Hakima:

In the first place, direct relations were established between Kuwait and the British East India company's representatives in the Gulf. Kuwait became important as a center for nearly all of the caravans carrying goods between Basrah and Allepo during the period 1775-1779. Because of the animosity existing between the British and the Persians, goods coming from India which could have been sent to Abu Shahr for conveyance to Allepo via Basrah, were unloaded at Zubara and Kuwait. This led to the accumulation of wealth at the two Utabi towns and the jealousy of other Arab seapowers.[3]

As a result of turmoil in the surrounding area, Kuwait declined as a commercial center during the years between 1790 and 1860. In 1793 and again in 1796 Kuwait was attacked by the Wahhabis from the interior; this fighting led to a decrease in the lucrative desert caravan trade. Meanwhile, the end of the Persian occupation of Basrah enabled that city to regain its commercial importance at Kuwait's expense. Although Kuwait's decline was only temporary, it demonstrated the impact that external factors would have upon the economy of the small city-state.

By the second half of the nineteenth century, Kuwait had regained its economic importance. Colonel Pelly, a British Resident in the Gulf who visited Kuwait in 1863 and 1865, gave this account of the reestablishment of its commercial activities:

Here is a clean town with broad and open bazaars and numerous solid stone dwelling houses stretching along the sand and containing some 20,000 inhabitants, attracting Arab and Persian merchants from all quarters, by the equity of its rule and by the freedom of its trade. . . The sailors of Kuwait are highly reputed and there may be some four thousand of them afloat. . . Horse forage comes in part down the Boobian Creek from Bunder Zobeir. Mutton, which is good, and mild butter, . . .[is received] . . . from the Bedouins, who flock the town and are pitched in tents or huts along the outside of the walls. Kuwait may boast of some 6,000 fighting men within its walls, but the policy has been to keep the peace internally and with all its neighbors.[4]

The increase in population from the 4,000 inhabitants noted by Stocqueler in 1832 indicates that the economic recovery of the town was in process. 'By 1860 Kuwait was the most important town on the Persian Gulf and attracted hundreds of crafts, owing to the healthy although severe climate, the friendliness of the inhabitants and the splendid anchorage.'[5]

The Pre-oil Economy of Kuwait

The pre-oil economy of Kuwait, like those of the rest of the Gulf, was based not on agriculture but mainly on trade, pearling, and fishing. It has been estimated that in the 1940s trade, seafaring, and pearling employed the major share of Kuwait's labor force of 8,000 to 10,000 men.[6]

The strategic location of Kuwait, enhanced by extensive Kuwaiti knowledge of the sea routes to India and Africa and a policy of minimal taxation, gave Kuwaiti merchants a good share of the Gulf trade. The trading season usually started in September and lasted for about ten months. Dates were the major commodity of trade and were loaded into deep-sea dhows in Basrah to be sold gradually in various ports of the coasts of the Gulf and India, and in the African ports of Lamu, Mombasa, and Zanzibar. Mangrove poles from Zanzibar were carried back home for use in construction. Smuggling was an essential part of the process:

> Dates taken on in Iraq are gradually sold off and the remainder declared cargos, such as: Persian rugs, bolts of cloth, and bags of sugar, bought in the markets of Kuwait and Aden, are disposed of. But, the real business of the captain and the crew is smuggling. It is the captain's opportunity for 'big profits' and the pay of the sailors is so little that they must make money by smuggling in order to live.[7]

The income of a ten-month trip was very meager indeed, especially for the sailor:

> The gross profit from a typical ten-month voyage is around 10,000 rupees. Once direct costs have been subtracted, about 4,000 rupees are left for the owners of the ship, and 4,000 rupees for division between the nokhoda (captain) and his

crew. The average Kuwaiti sailor feels that Allah has been good to him if he nets 150 rupees (50 dollars) for his ten months of tugging at ropes in the scorching sun and sleeping, drenched with dew, curled up on coils of rope. Most of this money may go for debts.[8]

The pearling season, which started in the summer and lasted for about three to four months, provided sailors with a second income to supplement their earnings from seafaring. A sailor's average earnings from a season's pearling amounted to an estimated 100 rupees (just over $35 at the pre-World War I rate),[9] a sum which hardly justified the suffering and risks that the divers incurred. The pearl industry flourished throughout the Gulf region, reaching its peak before World War I, when annual exports exceeded £2,000,000.[10] Around 1930, however, the industry suffered its greatest setback (from which it has never fully recovered) as a result of world-wide economic depression and the appearance on the market of Japanese cultured pearls. These events and the Saudi blockade precipitated a severe economic recession in Kuwait (another illustration of the vulnerability of its economy). This recession lasted until the commercial exploitation of oil transformed the country's economic foundation.

The annual pre-oil per capita income in Kuwait was lower than that in Iraq or Iran. 'Average family earnings from various sources barely touched 500 rupees (rather less than $180.00) a year. Assuming an average family of five, these calculations would suggest an average annual income of some 100 rupees (roughly about $35.00).'[11] These wages could be considered the lowest in the world, since they were paid to skilled workers. The situation was even worse, as far as unskilled workers were concerned. Their 'daily wage was not more than half a rupee, and employment was rarely available throughout the year.'[12] In sum, Kuwait's pre-oil economy had all the features of underdevelopment and backwardness.

The Coming of Oil

The first oil drilling in Kuwait was carried out by the Kuwait Oil Company (jointly owned by the Anglo-Persian Oil Company [now the British Petroleum Company Limited] and Gulf Oil Corporation) soon after it obtained a concession in 1934. The first well, which proved to be dry, was drilled in 1936 near a place known as Al-Bahara. The Burgan field, which was to become the principal source of Kuwait's crude oil, was discovered in 1938. The wells were plugged in 1942 due to the outbreak of World War II, and it was not until 1945 that drilling resumed. In 1946 commercial shipments of crude oil began flowing from the first terminal installation at Mina Al-Ahmadi. In that year Kuwait produced about 800,000 tons of crude oil; two years later, annual production was 7 million tons. During the Iranian oil crisis (1951-4),

Table 7.1: Total Crude Oil Production of Kuwait, 1946-77 (Millions of Barrels a Year)

Year	Oil Production	% Change
1946	5.9	—
1947	16.2	174.5
1948	46.5	187.03
1949	89.9	93.33
1950	125.7	39.8
1951	204.9	63.0
1952	273.4	33.4
1953	314.6	15.0
1954	349.8	11.18
1955	402.8	15.5
1956	405.5	0.67
1957	424.8	4.75
1958	522.4	23.0
1959	525.9	0.67
1960	619.2	17.74
1961	633.3	2.27
1962	714.6	12.83
1963	765.2	7.08
1964	842.2	10.06
1965	861.5	2.3
1966	906.7	5.24
1967	912.1	0.6
1968	952.2	4.81
1969	1,011.7	5.8
1970	1,090.6	7.8
1971	1,166.4	7.0
1972	1,201.6	3.0
1973	1,102.5	(8.3)
1974	929.4	(15.7)
1975	760.7	(18.15)
1976	785.0	3.09
1977	718.1	(8.5)

Source: Ministry of Oil, Kuwait, 1978.

production reached 47 million tons a year; in 1972, crude oil production in Kuwait hit a peak of over 1,200 million barrels. Table 7.1 shows oil production in millions of barrels per year and in annual percentage change from 1946 to 1977.

The fluctuating nature of Kuwait's oil production, largely a consequence of external factors, is evident in Table 7.1. This uncertainty has characterized the oil production schedules of many other oil-producing Gulf countries as well. Oil production was strongly affected by the policies of foreign oil companies as well as the political situation in other oil-producing countries.

This state of affairs continued until the mid-1960s and early 1970s, when Kuwait's parliament began to take a more active role in oil policy. This new dynamism on the part of the Kuwaiti government resulted in a participation agreement under whose terms the government acquired a 60 percent interest in the Kuwait Oil Company, thus paving the way for national control of the oil industry not only in Kuwait but in the rest of the Gulf oil-producing countries.

Government Expenditures

Until the government adopted a six-year plan in 1951, construction and development in Kuwait were ill-conceived and haphazard. Starting in the fiscal year 1960/1, Kuwait introduced a modern budgetary system to replace the *ad hoc* funds allocation procedures previously used.

One major budget item, especially in its early years, has been the land purchase program, adopted in 1952 for the purpose of achieving a just distribution of oil income among all of Kuwait's people. The result, unfortunately, did not fulfill the purpose of the program; land values increased at an unprecedented rate not only in Kuwait City but deep in the desert. The International Bank for Reconstruction and Development reported in 1965 that in the center of the city a piece of space just large enough for parking a car cost about KD 7,000.[13] Large tracts of worthless desert were seized and fenced in by those who had either the foresight or the foreknowledge to anticipate the coming public projects; they were subsequently compensated handsomely by the state. Because of the rapid turnover of land and the absence of legislation covering the acquisition of land for public use, the cost to the treasury was enormous.[14] During 1957-67 the total cost of the land puchase program was about KD 415.06 million; this accounted for 25 percent of total public expenditures and 24 percent of total oil revenues in the same period.

The government finally decided to reduce funding for the program from a peak level of KD 84.99 million in 1959-60 to KD 10 million in 1966-7. (By 1974-5 annual spending on the program had rebounded to a record high of KD 135 million; see Table 7.2.) The reduction undertaken in the 1960s was mainly due to the recommendation of the two missions of the International Bank for Reconstruction and Development to Kuwait in 1961 and 1963 respectively.

Many middle-income Kuwaitis invested heavily in land with bank loans during the period of speculation. Because of the decline of land prices that accompanied the cutback in the land purchase program, some of these investors went bankrupt. The government's policy of drastic rather than gradual cuts was severely criticized and created a partial recession in the country. The long-term effect of the land purchase program on the fabric of Kuwaiti society is well documented. The population became more dependent upon the government and lost some of its pre-oil entrepreneurial ability.[15] Similar processes have been at work in other oil-producing countries in the Gulf region. Land speculation reached its peak in Saudi Arabia, the United Arab Emirates, and Bahrain following the increase of oil prices in 1973.

Education and health rank high in Kuwaiti government expenditures. Prior to the oil era, governmental services in these sectors were very primitive. Expenditures on education increased from KD 83,800 in 1946-7 to more than KD 100 million in 1977. During the same period, the number of students in Kuwait's schools increased from 2,160 to 160,231; the number of teachers increased from 89 to 11,505. Because of inadequate planning at all levels of education, however, the system remains incapable of supplying the various sectors of the society with adequate manpower. Indeed, this lack of planning along with a lack of seriousness and motivation on the part of students has resulted in a noticeable decline in the quality of education.

Expenditures on health have also increased dramatically. Whereas in 1949 Kuwait had only one government hospital with 110 beds, in 1978 it had more than 10 hospitals with a total of about 4,418 beds. The number of doctors increased from 45 in

Table 7.2: Economic Classification of Government Expenditures, 1970-77 (KD Millions)

Year	Current	% of total	Development	% of total	Transfers	% of total	Land Purchase	% of total
1970-1	230.9	66.54	47.9	13.80	43.8	12.62	24.4	7.03
1971-2	276.3	73.77	50.7	13.53	41.8	11.16	19.9	1.53
1972-3	313.3	74.33	60.2	14.30	24.1	5.88	23.2	5.50
1973-4	438.4	78.62	73.2	13.13	20.9	3.74	25.1	4.50
1974-5	821.5	74.28	128.7	11.64	20.7	1.87	135.0	12.21
1975-6	834.9	72.64	203.2	17.68	22.0	1.91	89.2	7.76
1976-7	792.0	72.12	203.0	18.48	23.1	2.1	80.0	7.28

Source: Ministry of Finance, Kuwait, 1977.

1949 to some 1,478 in 1978. As in other small Gulf states, expenditures in other public service sectors such as housing, utilities, transport, and communications have reflected the government's eagerness to speed up the process of development; much of this effort has been characterized by waste. As a result of the 1979 revolution in Iran, however, this development (financed by surplus capital) has been slowed down in Kuwait and throughout the Gulf region.

Kuwaiti Foreign Policy

As is true for many other small states, security and survival have been the primary concerns of Kuwait's foreign policy. Throughout its history, Kuwait has attempted to maintain a local balance of power, to protect itself against tribal attacks, and to guarantee the security of its trade routes. Kuwait's rulers realized that neutrality provided the best guarantee for the continued existence of their small, weak state, and except during the protectorate period Kuwait's foreign policy has generally followed a neutral course.

Between 1896 and 1899, Kuwait found herself contending not only with local but with global powers. Germany and Russia were preparing to take their share of the colonial pickings. The backbone of the German colonial design in the Near and Middle East was the planned Baghdad Railway, which was intended (1) to strike a blow at British interests and influence in the eastern Mediterranean, Egypt, Mesopotamia, and India; and (2) to serve as an instrument to secure markets for Germany's growing industries. The main idea was to extend the European railway system through Asia Minor and down the Euphrates Valley to the Persian Gulf. Kuwait was chosen to be the terminus point. At the same time, Russian agents and travellers were observed in large numbers surveying possible sites for a coaling station and port. When a Russian cruiser was sent in 1900 to Bandar Abbas, the British reacted with panic (although it was soon realized that the Russians had no intention of occupying the port).

Increased German and Russian activities in the Gulf led to a more energetic British policy; British political and consular offices were subsequently established throughout the Gulf. This increase in British influence coincided with the assumption of power in Kuwait by Sheikh Mubarak Al-Sabah in 1896. Suspicious of

Turkish designs, Sheikh Mubarak sought British protection. Despite some initial British reluctance a treaty of protection was signed in 1899. In return for a British subsidy of about £1,000 per year, the sheikh obligated himself, his heirs, and his successors neither to cede, sell, lease, mortgage, nor give away for occupation or any other purpose any portion of his territory to the government or subject of any other power without the previous consent of the British government. Furthermore, Mubarak pledged to bind himself, his heirs, and his successors not to receive any foreign agents without the previous sanction of the British government. As if that was not enough, the 1899 agreement made Britain the formulator of Kuwait's foreign and defense policy. Similar treaties were also concluded between Britain and the other Gulf sheikhdoms.

The protectorate period lasted until 1961, when Kuwait gained its independence and once more entered the balance of power game within the Arab world and at the international level. As a newly independent state, Kuwait again treated security and survival as the primary policy goals — and not without reason. Only six days after Kuwait became independent from Britain, General Abdul-Karim Qasim, President of Iraq, laid claim to Kuwait. Kuwait reacted by declaring its determination to defend itself by every possible means, including invoking its assistance agreement with the United Kingdom. On July 1, 1961, Kuwait requested British military aid. Once more, Britain played a major role in preserving Kuwait's territorial integrity. Although the Iraqi threat was blocked, the dangers surrounding this immensely rich and vulnerable state still existed. It was thus determined that Kuwait should maintain military forces and seek to enlist Arab and international support in the event of a military attack.

Although Kuwait is weak militarily, since 1971 there has been considerable expansion of its military forces as a deterrent against potential aggressors. Between 1971 and 1977, Kuwait spent more than $3.5 billion on updating its defense capabilities; of this amount, $428 million was spent in 1977 alone. By 1977, defense expenditures accounted for about 35 percent of Kuwait's total national budget[16] and the percentage will presumably continue to rise. (For more on Kuwait's defense capacity, see Ch. 6.)

Kuwaiti Economic Assistance

Since 1953, Kuwait has been aiding the seven sheikhdoms that now make up the UAE. In December 1961, Kuwait established the Kuwait Fund for Arab Economic Development (KFAED), the initial purpose of which was to extend economic assistance to Arab states. It soon grew to become one of the largest financial institutions in the Third World. Its budget, which grew from KD 50 million in 1961 to KD 1 billion in 1974, constitutes 11.5 percent of Kuwait's annual national income. In relative terms, this is one of the largest foreign aid programs in the world. Over the period from its inception to 1980, the Kuwait Fund extended 142 loans totaling KD 590 million to 48 developing Arab, Asian, and African countries. Technical assistance grants are a new addition to the activities of the Fund; such grants have been extended to Guinea, the Maldives, and Rwanda.

Through Kuwait's state reserves, direct contributions have been

Table 7.3: State Reserves Loans to Arab Governments, 1958- 65

Borrower	Amount (KD Millions)	Date of Agreement	Duration of Loan (years)	Interest %
Dubai	0.400	12/11/58	10	3
	0.400	25/02/62	10	3.5
Jordan	1.000	18/07/60	10	4
	5.000	18/04/64	15	4
Lebanon	5.000	16/02/61	10	4
	5.000	23/05/65	15	4
Algeria	10.000	10/06/63	13	Nil
	10.000	25/04/65	15	4
Iraq	30.000	12/10/63	25	Nil
Egypt	3.000	02/12/63	12	Nil
	0.750	05/04/64	18	4
	25.000	12/04/64	15	4
	5.000	29/03/65	18	4
Tunisia	4.000	27/06/64	15	4
Morocco	10.000	26/04/65	15	4
Sudan	5.000	31/08/65	15	4
Yemen	0.250	21/06/65	N/A	Nil
Total	119.800			

Source: Ministry of Oil and Finance, Kuwait.

made to the Arab 'confrontation states' of Syria, Iraq, Jordan, and Egypt and the Palestine Liberation Organization. Loans from these reserves to Arab states between 1958 and 1965 totaled KD 119.8 million (see Table 7.3).

Following the outbreak of hostilities between Iran and Iraq in September 1980, Kuwait advanced an interest-free loan of $4 billion to Iraq; of this amount, $2 billion was granted in early 1981 prior to the election of Kuwait's revived parliament, and the remaining $2 billion was subsequently approved by parliament in a closed session.

Notes

1. For details of Kuwait's early history, see H.A. Al-Ebraheem, *Kuwait: A Political Study* (Kuwait: Kuwait University Press, 1975), pp. 23-4.

2. J.H. Stocqueler, *Fifteen Months' Pilgrimage Through Untrodden Tracts of Khuzistan and Persia in a Journey from India to England, Through Parts of Turkish Arabia, Armenia, Russia and Germany. Performed in the year 1831 and 1832* (London: Saunders and Otley, 1832).

3. A.H. Abu Hakima, *History of Eastern Arabia* (Beirut: Khayats, 1965), p. 96. The other city, Zubara, located in what is now called Qatar, is ruled by the Al-Khalifah family, the present rulers of Bahrain. They are a branch, along with Al-Jalahima, of the Utubi clan.

4. Quoted by H.J. Whigham, *The Persian Problem* (New York: Charles Scribner and Sons, 1903), p. 95.

5. C.A.P. Southwell, 'Kuwait,' *Journal of the Royal Society of Arts*, C11 24-41 (Dec. 11, 1953), p. 29.

6. See F. Shehab, 'Kuwait: A Super-Affluent Society,' *Foreign Affairs*, 42 (Apr. 1964), p. 463.

7. R.H. Sanger, *The Arabian Peninsula* (Ithaca: Cornell University Press, 1954), p. 157.

8. *Ibid.*, p. 163.

9. Shehab, 'Kuwait,' p. 463.

10. J.G. Lorimer, *Gazetteer of the Persian Gulf, Oman and Central Arabia*, Vol. 1 (Calcutta: Superintendent Government Printing, 1908-15) p. 164.

11. Shehab, 'Kuwait,' p. 463.

12. *Ibid.*, p. 463.

13. The International Bank for Reconstruction and Development, *The Economic Development of Kuwait* (Baltimore: The Johns Hopkins Press, 1965), p. 89.

14. Shehab, 'Kuwait,' p. 469.

15. R. El-Mallakh, *Economic Development and Regional Cooperation: Kuwait* (Chicago: Chicago University Press, 1968), p. 81.

16. *The Middle East*, No. 35 (Sept. 1977), p. 18.

8 CONCLUSION

Our examination of small states moved from generality to specificity, from consideration of small states throughout the world to scrutiny of the small states of the Arabian Gulf region. Our conclusion will follow the same pattern.

Although small states generally suffer from a variety of limitations, they are here to stay. Their proliferation in the United Nations is no cause for alarm, since small states can play an important mediating role in a world afflicted by cold-war tensions.

That small states should be active participants in world affairs is not a new phenomenon. Historically, small European states played a leading role in continental affairs. The Republic of Venice, with a population of less than 15,000, was a world power in the fifteenth century. Even such small states as Andorra, San Marino, Luxembourg, Liechtenstein, and Monaco were conceded their right to exist as independent states, and indeed participated in international conferences on an equal footing with larger states. For example, all states which participated in the Napoleonic wars, including the German and Italian micro- and mini-states, sent plenipotentiaries to the Congress of Vienna in 1814-15.

The uproar heard today about the increase of small states in the United Nations is nothing but a manifestation of the West's concern over the loss of its monopoly of power within the United Nations and other international organizations. In this connection, one cannot find a more eloquent statement in defense of smaller states than that made by the Prime Minister of Lesotho in a speech to the General Assembly in September 1967.

I at this stage venture to speak for all the smaller countries, including those which have recently been somewhat derisively categorized as the 'ministates.' Implicit in this description is the suggestion that they should forthwith surrender sovereignty and national identity and accept incorporation in some large political entity. I have three comments to make upon that view. The first, as I have already indicated, is that my people did not struggle for over a hundred years to achieve anonymity and oblivion. Second, I believe that such a view does not truly reflect the collective opinion of the Assembly and that it would violate the spirit and intention of the Charter. Thirdly, I believe that the smaller states have a specific and vital contribution to offer in the field of international relations.[1]

Small states must continue the struggle to survive, and their survival should be guaranteed by the international system through the United Nations.

If the existence of a small state is generally precarious, that of the small Gulf states, with their enticing wealth and oil, is even more so. The security formerly provided by the larger Arab states has been shattered by the controversy surrounding the Egyptian-Israeli peace accords, which left the Arab world divided and caused each country to engage in a struggle for its own survival. US–Israeli strategic cooperation accords negotiated in September 1981 have polarized the Arab world even further. This agreement also proved the failure, even before it started, of the US doctrine of so-called 'strategic consensus.' Shortly after Prime Minister Begin succeeded in obtaining an agreement with President Reagan, four Arab states — Libya, Syria, Algeria, and South Yemen — and the PLO declared their intention to develop a strategy of Arab-Soviet relations to counter-balance the US-Israeli accords. Thus, despite their major setbacks in the Arab world, the Russians now have a golden opportunity to reenter that region. This Arab agreement, however limited, reflects a growing polarization in the Arab world between allies of the Soviet Union and those willing to cooperate with US Middle East policies — policies which are based on the US obsession with East-West conflict and which ignore some basic issues of the area. The present US approach, then, can only bring more Soviet involvement in the region and undermine the vital interests of the United States and Western Europe.

The case of Kuwait, examined in the last chapter, exemplifies the fear felt by small states standing alone in an area of superpower confrontation. Kuwait departed from 250 years of local neutrality when it initiated the Gulf Cooperation Council, but this policy of alliance as a step toward the eventual full integration reflects the recognition on the part of Kuwait and the other Gulf states that they cannot survive on an individual basis. This approach to the problem of security is not unique. Only four years after gaining its independence from Britain in 1959,

Singapore joined the Federation of Malaysia.[2] (However, because of ethnic tensions between Malayans and Chinese, the Federation ended in 1965.)

The question remains whether the Gulf states can survive even with the Cooperation Council. As was pointed out earlier in this book, alliances with more powerful states cannot guarantee the security of small states. They can, however, move toward federation with some degree of success through policies of integration provided that they have no built-in ethnic time bombs such as that which undermined the Malaysian Federation.

In the case of the Gulf states, the road toward unification is not an easy one. In spite of a common culture, language, ethnicity, and historical background, serious obtacles must be overcome. These include not only unsolved border problems but family competition among the ruling dynasties. Beyond these difficulties lies the grave threat posed by superpower maneuvering. Moreover, intelligent decision-making in the Gulf states requires a full awareness that in the Arab world there is a staggering uneven distribution of wealth between the 'have' and 'have-not' states. While the average GNP per capita for the Arab world was slightly over $1,000 per annum in the late 1970s, the rich states — Kuwait, the United Arab Emirates, Libya, Qatar, and Saudi Arabia — enjoy a per capita income close to that of the United States. Yet these states represent no more than 6 percent of the total population of the Arab world. The poorer Arab countries —Yemen, Egypt, Sudan, Mauritania, and Somalia — contain 50 percent of the entire Arab population and had a joint per capita income of about $320 per annum in the late 1970s.[3] Economically weak and overpopulated Arab states can present grave dangers to the Cooperation Council, the success of which will depend largely on its ability to create a new economic order based on equality and justice. But the increase in defense spending in the Gulf states seems to indicate that no common strategy has been adopted to channel funds into general Arab development. If we consider only one member of the Council, Saudi Arabia, we find that its defense spending rose from $171 million in 1968 to $13,170 million in 1978, or more than 7,600 percent in one decade. Saudi Arabia's per capita defense expenditure was $1,704 compared with Algeria's $25, Egypt's $112, Iraq's $141, Iran's $224, and Israel's $887.[4] Not only does such expenditure by the Gulf states represent a waste of precious resources but it signals heavy reliance on foreign powers and an unfair recycling of petrodollars back to the industrial West.

All six Gulf Cooperation Council members suffer from a lack of indigenous skilled manpower. They can neither man their highly sophisticated weaponry nor even maintain it. Further, most of the arms purchased from the West are not essential to the defense needs of the various countries but rather are acquired for the sake of national prestige. Here a lesson might be drawn from Iran, where the Shah stockpiled sophisticated weaponry, but high performance could not be achieved. The Iranian navy, for instance, always suffered from lack of skilled manpower and its readiness was not highly rated. If this was the case with Iran, the situation in the small states of the Gulf is probably even worse because of their smaller indigenous populations. It can therefore be concluded that heavy emphasis upon armaments will, in the long run, constitute a disruptive force causing serious economic and political problems without adding to the real security of the Gulf governments. Not only will this unwarranted importation of armaments contribute to the destabilization of the region, but it will open it to direct intervention from both the West and the East.

Integration efforts in the Gulf should be viewed as a first step toward integration among Arab countries in general. The tragic events that all Arab people have endured should spur them to work all the harder to build a federation capable of withstanding the challenge now confronting them, a challenge which threatens their very survival as a nation. If the Gulf Cooperation Council is to become the seed of a wider Arab federation, its first order of business must be a clear policy declaration, based on neutrality, opposing all foreign military bases in the Gulf. The West must also be made to understand that the security of oil supplies depends essentially upon reaching a peaceful settlement of the Arab-Israeli crisis, and that this must include a just solution of the Palestinian problem. The Council must strive to reduce the gap between the rich and poor in the Arab world. This could be done through the adoption of a plan similar to the US Marshall Plan which revived the shattered European economies following World War II. While these steps must be taken on the regional and international levels, internally there must be a commitment to justice and equality. An immediate move toward democratization of the various regimes represented on the Council should be undertaken according to a fixed timetable. An end to corruption, nepotism, and sexual segregation within these societies must be achieved. An open door policy with respect to the naturalization of Arab expatriates must be adopted. These are only a few of the major challenges facing the Gulf Cooperation Council. Whether the Gulf countries can meet these challenges will determine their ultimate prospects of survival.

Notes

1. United Nations, General Assembly, verbatim records, A/PV. 1565, p. 11 (Sept. 25, 1967).
2. Singapore is a relatively wealthy state, with standards in health, education, and housing that are among the highest in Asia.
3. S. Ibrahim, 'Superpowers in the Arab World,' *Washington Quarterly*, Vol. 4, No. 3 (Summer 1981), p. 82.
4. Quoted in *ibid.*, p. 91.

BIBLIOGRAPHY

Abu Hakima, A.H. *History of Eastern Arabia*. Beirut: Khayats, 1965.

Albharna, H.M. *The Arabian Gulf States*. Beirut: Librairie du Liban, 1975.

Benedict, Burton, ed. *Problems of Smaller Territories*. London: The Athlone Press, 1967. Published for the Institute of Commonwealth Studies.

Bhutto, Ali *The Myth of Independence*. London: Oxford University Press, 1969.

Birks, J.S. and C.A. Sinclair *Arab Manpower: The Crisis of Development*. New York: St Martin's Press, 1980.

Blechman, B.M. and S.S. Kaplan *Force Without War: U.S. Armed Forces as a Political Instrument*. Washington, DC: The Brookings Institution, 1978.

Bull, H. *The Anarchical Society*. London: Macmillan, 1977.

Carr, E.H. *The Bolshevik Revolution 1917-1923*, Vol. 1. London: Macmillan, 1964.

Clark, R.W. *The Greatest Power on Earth*. New York: Harper and Row, 1980.

Cohen, S.B. 'The Emergence of a New Second Order of Powers in the International System,' *Nuclear Proliferation and the Nuclear Countries*, ed. Marwah and Schulz. Cambridge: Ballinger, 1976.

Copley, Gregory R., ed. *Defense and Foreign Affairs Handbook*. Washington, DC: Copley and Associates, S.A., 1981.

Dawisha, A.I. *Egypt in the Arab World*. New York: John Wiley and Sons, 1976.

Deutsch, K.W. *The Nerves of Government*. New York: Free Press, 1963.

—— 'Security Communities,' *International Politics and Foreign Policy*, ed. J.N. Rosenan. New York: The Free Press of Glencoe, 1961.

Al-Ebraheem, H.A. *Kuwait: A Political Study*. Kuwait: Kuwait University Press, 1975.

Emerson, R. *From Empire to Nation*. Cambridge: Harvard University Press, 1960.

Farran, C. D'Olivier 'The Position of Diminutive States in International Law,' *International Rechtliche und Staatsrechtliche Abhandlungen*. Dusseldorf: Hermes, 1960.

Fox, Annette Baker *The Power of Small States: Diplomacy in World War II*. Chicago: University of Chicago Press, 1959.

Friedrich, C.J. *Trends of Federalism in Theory and Practice*. London: Pall Mall, 1968.

Good, Robert 'State-Building as Determinant of Foreign Policy in the New States,' *Neutralism and Non-Alignment: The New States in World Affairs*, ed. L. Martin. New York: Praeger, 1962.

Haas, E. *The Uniting of Europe*. Reissued, with a new preface. Stanford: Stanford University Press, 1968.

Hansen, R.D. *Beyond the North-South Stalemate*. New York: McGraw-Hill, 1979.

Hill, Christopher 'Theories of Foreign Policy Making for the Developing Countries,' *Foreign Policy Making in Developing States*, ed. Christopher Clapham. London: Saxon House, 1977.

Hull, C. *The Memoirs of Cordell Hull*. New York: Macmillan, 1948. (2 Vols.)

Hunter, Robert H. *The Soviet Dilemma in the Middle East, Part II: Oil and the Persian Gulf*. London: The International Institute for Strategic Studies, 1969. Adelphi Papers No. 60.

The International Bank for Reconstruction and Development *The Economic Development of Kuwait*. Baltimore: The Johns Hopkins Press, 1965.

Issawi, C. and M. Yeganeh *The Economics of Middle East Oil*. New York: Praeger, 1962.

Kaplan, S.S. *Diplomacy of Power: Soviet Armed Forces as a Political Instrument*. Washington, DC: The Brookings Institution, 1981.

Kelly, J.B. *Arabia, the Gulf, and the West: A Critical View of the Arabs and Their Oil Policy*. London: Weidenfeld and Nicolson, 1980.

Kissinger, H.A. *American Foreign Policy*, Expanded edn. New York: N.W. Norton and Co., Inc., 1974.

Kuznets, S. 'Economic Growth of Small Nations,' *Economic Consequences of the Size of Nations*, ed. E.A.G. Robinson. New York: St Martin's Press, 1960.

Leeman, W.A. *The Price of Middle East Oil*. Ithaca: Cornell University Press, 1962.

Lorimer, J.G. *Gazetteer of the Persian Gulf, Oman and Central Arabia*. Vol. 1. Calcutta: Superintendent Government Printing, 1908-15.

El-Mallakh, R. *Economic Development and Regional Cooperation: Kuwait*. Chicago: Chicago University Press, 1968.

Marlowe, J. *The Persian Gulf in the Twentieth Century*. London: The Crescent Press, 1962.

Myrdal, Gunnar *Asian Drama, An Inquiry into the Poverty of Nations*. 3 Vols. New York: Pantheon Books, 1968.

Newsom, D.D. 'United States Policy Toward the Gulf,' *The United States, Arabia, and the Gulf*, ed. R.G. Wolfe. Washington, DC: Center for Contemporary Arab Studies (Georgetown University), 1980.

Nkrumah, K. *Neo-Colonialism: The Last Stage of Imperialism*. New York: International Publishers, 1965.

O'Connor, James 'The Meaning of Economic Imperialism,' *Readings in U.S. Imperialism*, eds. K.T. Fann and D.C. Hodges. Boston: Porter Sargent, 1971.

Oxaal, I. *Black Intellectuals Come to Power*. Cambridge, Massachusetts: Schenkman, 1967.

Pearson, Lester *Democracy in World Politics*. Princeton, NJ: Princeton University Press, 1956.

Rawlinson, G. *Ancient History from the Earliest Times to the Fall of the Western Empire*. New York: Colonial Press, 1900.

Reischauer, E.O. *Japan: Past and Present*. New York: Knopf, 1946.

Rothstein, R.L. *Alliances and Small Powers*. New York: Columbia University Press, 1968.

Said, E.W. *Covering Islam: How the Media and the Experts Determine How We See the Rest of the World*. New York: Pantheon Books, 1981.

—— *The Question of Palestine*. New York: Vintage Books, 1980.

Sanger, R.H. *The Arabian Peninsula*. Ithaca: Cornell University Press, 1954.

Sayegh, Youssef *The Economics of the Arab World: Development Since 1945*. New York: St Martin's Press, 1978.

Servan-Schreiber, Jean-Jacques *The World Challenge*. New York: Simon and Schuster, 1981.

El-Sheikh, R. *Kuwait: Economic Growth of the Oil States, Problems and Policies*. Kuwait: Kuwait University Press, 1972.

Singer, M. *Weak States in a World of Powers*. New York: Free

Press, 1972.

Singham, A.W. *The Hero and the Crowd in the Colonial Polity.* New Haven: Yale University Press, 1967.

Snyder, R.C., H.W. Bruck, and B. Spain *Decision-Making as an Approach to the Study of International Politics.* Princeton: Princeton University Press, 1954. Foreign Policy Analysis, Series 3.

Stocqueler, J.H. *Fifteen Months' Pilgrimage Through Untrodden Tracts of Khuzistan and Persia in a Journey from India to England Through Parts of Turkish Arabia, Armenia, Russia and Germany, Performed in the Year 1831 and 1832.* London: Saunders and Otley, 1832.

Sveics, V.V. *Small Nation Survival.* New York: Exposition Press, 1969.

Svennilson, I. 'The Concept of the Nation and its Relevance to Economic Analysis,' *Economic Consequences of the Size of Nations,* ed. E.A.G. Robinson. New York: St Martin's Press, 1960.

Taylor, Charles 'Statistical Typology of Micro-States and Territories,' *Small States and Territories: Status and Problems,* eds. J. Rapoport, E. Muteba, and J.J. Therattil. New York: Arno Press, 1971, pp. 183-202. A UNITAR study.

Van Wagenen, Richard W. *Research in the International Organization Field: Some Notes on Possible Focus.* Princeton: Center for Research on World Political Institutions, 1952.

Vital, David *The Inequality of States: A Study of Small Power in International Relations.* Oxford: Clarendon Press, 1967.

Whigham, H.J. *The Persian Problem.* New York: Charles Scribner and Sons, 1903.

Williams, William A. *Empire as a Way of Life.* Oxford: Oxford University Press, 1981.

York, H.F. 'Nuclear Deterrence: How to Reduce the Overkill,' *Pacem in Terris III,* ed. F.W. Neal and M.K. Harvey. Vol. 2. Santa Barbara, California: Center for the Study of Democratic Institutions, 1974.

Periodicals

Ajami, F. 'Retreat from Economic Nationalism: The Political Economy of Sadat's Egypt,' *Journal of Arab Affairs,* Vol. 1, No. 1 (Oct. 1981), p. 44.

Ajayi, J.F.A. 'The Place of African History and Culture in the

Process of Nation-Building in Africa South of the Sahara,' *Journal of Negro Education*, 30 (1961), p. 202.

Bloomfield, A.I. and R.C. Marson 'Policies for an OPEC Dollar Run,' *Journal of Post-Keynesian Economics*, Vol. III, No. 3, (Spring 1981), pp. 300-2.

Cambon, Jules 'The Permanent Basis of French Foreign Policy,' *Foreign Affairs*, 8 (1930), p. 174.

The Economist, May 21, 1966, p. 803.

The Economist Intelligence Unit *Quarterly Economic Review of Kuwait*, 2nd Quarter, 1981, p. 4.

East, Maurice A. 'Size and Foreign Policy Behavior: A Test of Two Models,' *World Politics*, 25 (1973), p. 557.

—— 'Foreign Policy Making in Small States: Some Theoretic Observations Based on the Study of Uganda's Foreign Ministry,' *Policy Science*, 4 (Dec. 1973), pp. 491-508.

Al-Ebraheem, H.A. and R.P. Stevens 'Organization, Management and Academic Problems in the Arab University: The Kuwait University Experience,' *Higher Education*, 9 (1980), pp. 203-18.

Ehrlich, T. And C. Gwin 'A Third World Strategy,' *Foreign Policy*, No. 44 (Autumn 1981), pp. 145-66.

Fisher, R. 'The Participation of Ministates in International Affairs,' *American Society of International Law* (1968), p. 168.

Fulbright, J.W. 'Another Tonkin Gulf?', *Washington Post*, August 23, 1981, C-8.

Harbert, J.R. 'The Behavior of the Mini-States in the United Nations, 1971-1972,' *International Organization*, 30 (Winter 1976), pp. 109-27.

Holsti, J.K. 'Retreat from Utopia: International Relations Theory, 1945-70,' *Canadian Journal of Political Science*, Vol IV, No. 2 (June 1971), p. 174.

Ibrahim, S. 'Superpowers in the Arab World,' *Washington Quarterly*, Vol. 4, No. 3 (Summer 1981), pp. 81-94.

Kawari, A.K. 'Haqiqat al-tanmiah al-naftiah,' *Al-Mustaqbal Al-Arabi*, No. 27 (May 1981), pp. 34-45. Published monthly by the Center for Arab Unity Studies in Beirut.

Keohane, R.O. 'Lilliputian's Dilemmas: Small States in International Politics,' *International Organization*, 23 (1969), p. 296.

M.H. Kerr 'Rich and Poor in the New Arab Order,' *Journal of Arab Affairs*. Vol. No. 1 (Oct. 1981), pp. 1-24.

Kuwait News Agency, *Digest*, 'The Gulf Cooperation Council,'

February 16, 1981, pp. 67-76.

—— *Digest*, 'The Gulf Cooperation Council,' May 1981, pp. 8-9 and p. 79.

Lissakers, K. 'Money Manipulation,' *Foreign Policy*, No. 44 (Fall 1981), pp. 107-26.

Lockhart, L. 'Outline of the History of Kuwait,' *Journal of the Royal Central Asian Society*, 34 (July–Oct. 1947), p. 262.

The Middle East (Sept. 1977), p. 18.

Oil and Gas Journal, BP Statistical Review of the World Oil Industry, 1981.

Ott, Marvin, C. 'Foreign Policy Formulation in Malaysia,' *Asian Survey*, 12 (1972), pp. 225-91.

Plimpton, F.T.O. 'The United Nations Needs Family Planning,' *The New York Times Magazine*, September 18, 1966, p. 97.

Ramazani, R.K. 'Security in the Persian Gulf,' *Foreign Affairs*, 57 (Spring 1979), pp. 824-5.

Rapoport, J.G. 'The Participation of Ministates in International Affairs,' *Proceedings, American Society of International Law* (1968), pp. 156-7.

Shehab, F. 'Kuwait: A Super-Affluent Society,' *Foreign Affairs*, 42 (Apr. 1964), p. 463.

Southwell, C.A.P. 'Kuwait,' *Journal of the Royal Society of Arts*, C11 24-41 (Dec. 11, 1953), p. 29.

Sprout, Harold and Margaret 'The Dilemma of Rising Demands and Insufficient Resources,' *World Politics*, 20 (1968), pp. 660-93.

Swearingen, W.D. 'Sources of Conflict Over Oil in the Persian/Arabian Gulf,' *The Middle East Journal*, Vol. 35, No. 3 (Summer 1981), pp. 315-30.

Szulc, Tad 'The Unthinkable,' *The Washingtonian*, Vol. 16, No. 9 (June 1981), pp. 106-15.

Tucker, R.W. 'Oil: The Issues of American Intervention,' *Commentary*, 59 (January 1975), pp. 21-31.

Vayrynen, Raimo 'On the Definition and Measurement of Small Power States,' *Cooperation and Conflict: Nordic Journal of International Politics*, 62 (1971), p. 99.

Vellut, Jean-Luc 'Small States and the Problem of War and Peace: Some Consequences of the Emergence of Smaller States in Africa,' *Journal of Peace Research*, No. 4 (1967), p. 254.

Villierars, A. 'Some Aspects of the Arab Dhow Trade,' *The Middle East Journal*, Vol. 2, No. 4 (Oct. 1948), p. 399.

Von Crevald, M. 'Turning Points in Twentieth Century War,' *Washington Quarterly*, Vol. 4, No. 3 (Summer 1981), p. 7.

Von Kuhlmann, R. 'The Permanent Basis of German Foreign Policy,' *Foreign Affairs*, 9 (1931), p. 179.

Whitaker, U. 'Mini-Membership for Mini-States,' *War and Peace Report*, Vol. 7, No. 3 (Apr. 1967), p. 3.

Wiesner, J.B. and H.F. York. 'National Security and the Nuclear Test Ban,' *Scientific American*, Vol. 229, No. 4 (Oct. 1964), p. 24.

Reports, Documents, etc.

Blair, Patricia Wohlgemuth *The Mini-State Dilemma*, Occasional Paper No. 6, Carnegie Endowment for International Peace (Oct. 1967), p. 3.

Center for Strategic and International Studies (Georgetown University) *The Gulf: Implications of British Withdrawal*, Georgetown University, 1969, pp. 7-8.

The Global 2000 Report to the President, Vol. 1 (Washington, DC: 1981), p. 1.

Hammerstein, Oscar 2nd and Richard Rodgers 'A Puzzlement,' *The King and I*, copyright (c) 1951 by Williamson Music, Inc.

Long, D.E. *Confrontation and Cooperation in the Gulf* (Washington, DC: Middle East Institute, 1974), Middle East Problem Paper.

Oburdene, O. 'The Investment Income of Saudi Arabia and Kuwait' (June 1981).

Stockholm International Peace Research Institute Yearbook, 1975, p. 100.

US Arms Control and Disarmament Agency, *World Military Expenditures and Arms Transfers, 1970-1979*, US Government Printing Office, Washington, DC, 1980.

United Nations General Assembly, Verbatim records, A/PV, 1565, September 25, 1961, p. 11.

US Congressional Documents

US House of Representatives, Committee on Foreign Affairs *New Perspectives on the Persian Gulf Hearings, Subcommittee on the Near East and South Asia*, 93rd congress, 1st session, 1973 (Washington, DC: US Government Printing Office, 1973).

US House of Representatives, Committee on Foreign Affairs *US Security Interests in the Persian Gulf: Report of a Staff Study*

Mission to the Persian Gulf, Middle East and Horn of Africa, October 21–November 13, 1980 (Washington, DC: US Government Printing Office, 1981).

US House of Representatives, Committee on International Relations *The Persian Gulf, 1975: The Continuing Debate on Arms Sales. Hearings, Special Subcommittee on Investigations*, 94th Congress, 1st Session, 1975 (Washington, DC: US Government Printing Office, 1976).

US Senate *The Salt II Treaty, Report of the Committee on Foreign Relations, US Senate* (Washington, DC: US Government Printing Office, 1979).

INDEX